HANDBOOK FOR DEVELOPING JOINT CREDITING MECHANISM PROJECTS

ASIAN DEVELOPMENT BANK

50 YEARS

ADB

© 2016 Asian Development Bank
6 ADB Avenue, Mandaluyong City, 1550 Metro Manila, Philippines
Tel +63 2 632 4444; Fax +63 2 636 2444
www.adb.org

Some rights reserved. Published in 2016.
Printed in the Philippines.

ISBN 978-92-9257-717-9 (Print), 978-92-9257-718-6 (e-ISBN)
Publication Stock No. TIM168063-2

Cataloging-In-Publication Data

Asian Development Bank.
        Handbook for developing joint crediting mechanism projects.
Mandaluyong City, Philippines: Asian Development Bank, 2016.

1. Joint Crediting Mechanism.   2. Asian Development Bank.   I. Asian Development Bank.

The views expressed in this publication are those of the authors and do not necessarily reflect the views and policies of the Asian Development Bank (ADB) or its Board of Governors or the governments they represent.

ADB does not guarantee the accuracy of the data included in this publication and accepts no responsibility for any consequence of their use. The mention of specific companies or products of manufacturers does not imply that they are endorsed or recommended by ADB in preference to others of a similar nature that are not mentioned.

By making any designation of or reference to a particular territory or geographic area, or by using the term "country" in this document, ADB does not intend to make any judgments as to the legal or other status of any territory or area.

Notes:
1. In this publication, "$" refers to US dollars.
2. ADB recognizes "China" as the People's Republic of China and "Vietnam" as Viet Nam.
Corrigenda to ADB publications may be found at http://www.adb.org/publications/corrigenda

Printed on recycled paper

CONTENTS

TABLES, FIGURES, AND BOXES

Tables

Figures

Boxes

FOREWORD

The Asian Development Bank (ADB) established its Carbon Market Program (CMP) in 2006 that continues to provide technical support and carbon finance to greenhouse gas (GHG) mitigation activities in its developing member countries (DMCs). The CMP includes (i) the Asia Pacific Carbon Fund, (ii) the Future Carbon Fund, (iii) the Japan Fund for the Joint Crediting Mechanism, and (iv) the Technical Support Facility (TSF). The TSF has been the main instrument through which ADB provides capacity building support to its DMCs for enhancing mitigation actions through carbon markets.

Building on ADB's strong expertise and experience in implementing previous technical assistance projects under the TSF, a regional capacity development technical assistance was designed to support DMCs in accessing carbon finance through new carbon market mechanisms, especially bilateral mechanisms such as the Joint Crediting Mechanism (JCM).

Initiated by the Government of Japan, JCM is a bilateral offset crediting mechanism with an objective to facilitate implementation of advanced low-carbon technologies that can mitigate GHG emissions in the host countries.

The Paris Agreement, which was adopted in December 2015 and came in force in November 2016, signifies hope for the resurgence of carbon markets since it establishes the international policy infrastructure required to support carbon markets, at a domestic, regional and international level. Under Article 6(2), the Paris Agreement allows countries to voluntarily cooperate in meeting their nationally determined contributions by using "cooperative approaches," which may well spur further development of bilateral mechanisms such as the JCM.

This handbook was developed under the technical assistance for *Supporting the Use of Carbon Financing from New Carbon Market Mechanisms to Promote Green Growth in Asia and the Pacific,* to provide project participants and other stakeholders practical guidance to develop JCM projects by taking the reader through each of the procedural steps of the JCM project development cycle that lead up to the issuance of JCM credits.

Ma. Carmela D. Locsin
Director General
Sustainable Development and Climate Change Department
Asian Development Bank

ACKNOWLEDGMENTS

This handbook draws on the knowledge product, *Joint Crediting Mechanism: An Emerging Bilateral Crediting Mechanism*, which provides information on bilateral mechanisms with specific reference to the Joint Crediting Mechanism (JCM). It is a collaborative effort of the members of the Technical Support Facility, a component of the Carbon Market Program of the Sustainable Development and Climate Change Department (SDCC) of the Asian Development Bank (ADB). It has been prepared under the regional technical assistance for *Supporting the Use of Carbon Financing from New Carbon Market Mechanisms to Promote Green Growth in Asia and the Pacific*.

Ma. Carmela D. Locsin, director general, SDCC, encouraged the development of this handbook for use by project developers in ADB's developing member countries. Preety Bhandari, director, Climate Change and Disaster Risk Management Division (SDCD), provided overall guidance, and Virender K. Duggal, principal climate change specialist (SDCD, SDCC), supervised the development of this handbook.

The preparation of this handbook was made possible by the valuable contributions and technical inputs from; Ayato Kurokawa, climate finance specialist (consultant); Raymond Caguioa, carbon market expert (consultant); Takeshi Miyata, climate finance specialist (consultant); Kate Hughes, climate finance specialist (consultant); Muhammad Irfan Pawennei, carbon market expert (consultant); Shaymal Barman, carbon market expert (consultant); Ha Son, carbon market expert (consultant); Hanh Le, carbon market expert (consultant); and Jose Alfred Cantos, technical assistance coordinator (consultant).

ABBREVIATIONS

BAU	–	business as usual
CAR	–	corrective action request
CDM	–	Clean Development Mechanism
CL	–	clarification request
COP	–	coefficient of performance
CO_2	–	carbon dioxide
CSPF	–	cooling seasonal performance factor
DMC	–	developing member country
EER	–	energy efficiency ratio
EIA	–	environmental impact assessment
FAR	–	forward action request
GHG	–	greenhouse gas
HOB	–	heat only boiler
ISO	–	International Organization for Standardization
JCM	–	Joint Crediting Mechanism
JFJCM	–	Japan Fund for the Joint Crediting Mechanism
kW	–	kilowatt
kWh	–	kilowatt-hour
LCA	–	life cycle analysis
MOC	–	modalities of communication statement
MPS	–	monitoring plan sheet
MRS	–	monitoring report sheet
MRV	–	monitoring, reporting, and verification
MW	–	megawatt
MWh	–	megawatt-hour
NEDO	–	New Energy and Industrial Technology Development Organization
PDD	–	project design document
PMS	–	proposed methodology spreadsheet
QA/QC	–	quality assurance and quality control
RAC	–	room air conditioner
SDIP	–	sustainable development implementation plan
tCO_2e	–	tons of carbon dioxide equivalent
TPE	–	third-party entity

INTRODUCTION

Purpose

The purpose of this handbook is to provide project participants and relevant stakeholders with information on how to develop a Joint Crediting Mechanism (JCM) project. The handbook can be used for potential project participants who are considering developing JCM projects, or project participants that have developed, or in the process of developing JCM projects. The handbook provides step-by-step guidance on how to develop a project in order to successfully achieve registration, and qualify to receive JCM credits.

Target Audience

The target audience for this handbook are potential and existing project participants. This handbook will also be useful for stakeholders within the carbon market that are interested in the JCM and how the JCM project cycle works.

References

This handbook has been prepared using official JCM documents approved by the Joint Committee of respective host countries. This includes, but is not limited to: *Rules of Implementation for the Joint Crediting Mechanism; Joint Crediting Mechanism Project Cycle Procedure; Joint Crediting Mechanism Guidelines for Developing Proposed Methodology; Joint Crediting Mechanism Guidelines for Developing Project Design Document and Monitoring Report; and Joint Crediting Mechanism Guidelines for Validation and Verification.* The handbook also refers to approved methodologies, project design documents, monitoring reports, validation reports, and verification reports. Specific documents are referenced throughout this guide, and official JCM documents can also be found on the JCM website of each host country, accessed at https://www.jcm.go.jp/

Latest Information

This handbook has been prepared based on the JCM rules and guidelines that are common to all host countries. To date, the rules and guidelines have largely been identical among all the JCM host countries in Asia and the Pacific. However, each Joint Committee in each host country has the authority to set its own rules and guidelines to implement the JCM in their country. It is therefore recommended that the project participants check with their country's Joint Committee for the latest rules and guidelines prior to commencing a JCM project.

MODULE 1:
OVERVIEW OF THE JOINT CREDITING MECHANISM

1.1   INTRODUCTION TO THE MODULE

Module 1 provides an introduction to the Joint Crediting Mechanism (JCM).[1] It explains what the JCM is, how it works and who the key stakeholders are. This module is divided into five subsections: (1.1) Introduction to the Module, (1.2) Objectives and Concepts, (1.3) Stakeholders and Governance Structure, (1.4) Rules and Guidelines, and (1.5) JCM Eligible Project Types.

1.2   OBJECTIVES AND CONCEPTS

1.2.1   Objectives

The JCM aims to facilitate the diffusion of leading low-carbon technologies, products, systems, services, and infrastructure resulting in the mitigation of greenhouse gas (GHG) emissions. JCM projects also contribute to the sustainable development and GHG reduction efforts of the host countries. The GHG emission reductions or removals achieved through the JCM projects are intended to be used by Japan, and the host countries, to achieve their respective GHG emission reduction targets.

1.2.2   Relationship between Japan and host country

JCM projects are implemented through bilateral agreements between Japan and individual host countries. As of September 2016, 16 countries have signed these bilateral agreements. The resulting GHG emission reductions that meet all of the requirements of the JCM process may be credited to the project participants of both participating countries. In this way, Japan and the host country will be able to use their portion of JCM credits towards their GHG emission reduction target. Japan can also provide financing for JCM projects through various financing schemes (outlined in Section 1.3).

Figure 1.1 shows an overview of the scheme between Japan and each host country.

---

[1]   The mechanism was first launched as the Bilateral Offset Credit Mechanism, but it is now more commonly called the Joint Crediting Mechanism or the JCM.

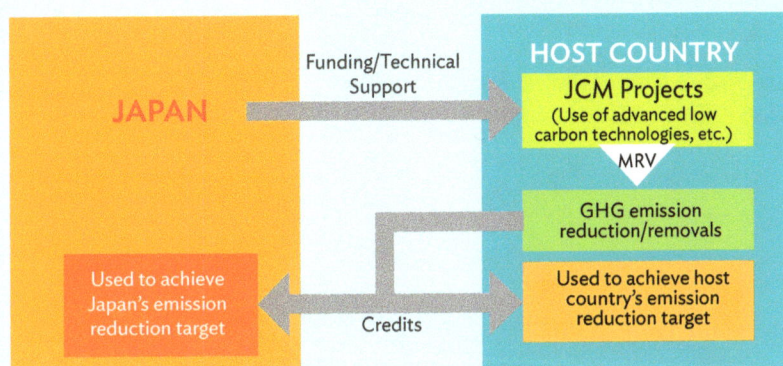

Figure 1.1: Overview of the Joint Crediting Mechanism Scheme

GHG = greenhouse gas, JCM = Joint Crediting Mechanism, MRV = monitoring, reporting, and verification.

Source: Adapted from Government of Japan documents.

1.2.3 Concept of calculating emission reductions

The JCM was designed to take into consideration robust methodologies, transparency, and environmental integrity of its procedures, rules, and guidelines, while maintaining simplicity and practicality. Under the JCM, emission reductions are calculated as the difference between "reference emissions" and "project emissions." Reference emissions are set at emissions estimated below business-as-usual (BAU) level. The details of calculating emission reductions are discussed in Module 3.

1.2.4 Preventing double counting of emissions

JCM procedures also address potential double counting of emission reductions by establishing registries in each host country and Japan, to track issued credits and corresponding registry account details. The use of these registries will also prevent registered JCM projects from being used under any other international climate mitigation mechanisms.

1.2.5 Total greenhouse gas emission reductions to date

As of September 2016, there are 15 registered JCM projects with a potential to reduce 3,332 tons of carbon dioxide (tCO_2) annually. The full list of registered projects can be found in Appendix 1.

1.3   STAKEHOLDERS AND GOVERNANCE STRUCTURE

Figure 1.2 provides an overview of the various stakeholders involved in the JCM and their interface during the implementation of a JCM project.

Figure 1.2: Joint Crediting Mechanism Stakeholders and Roles

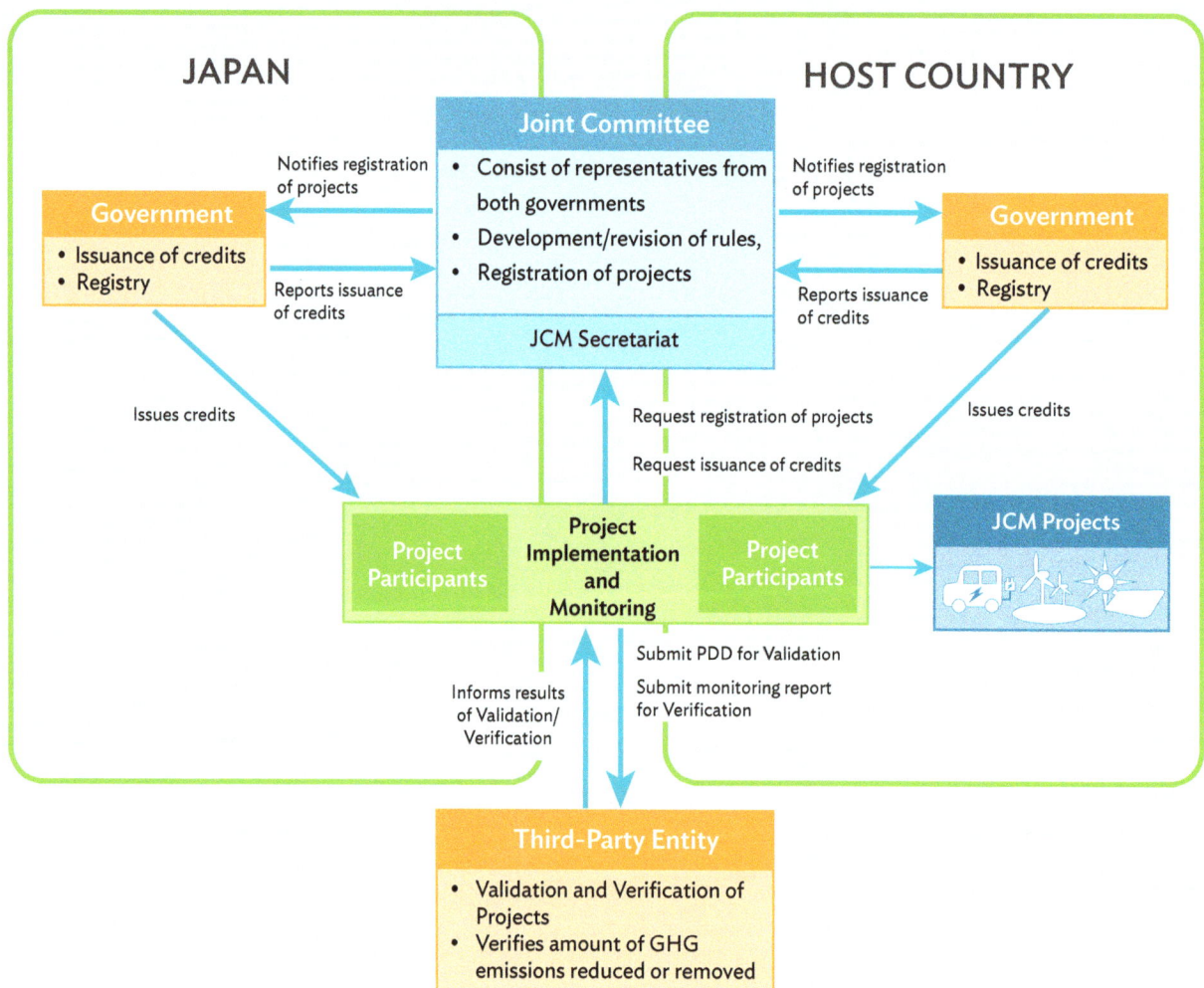

JAPAN

HOST COUNTRY

Joint Committee
- Consist of representatives from both governments
- Development/revision of rules,
- Registration of projects

JCM Secretariat

Notifies registration of projects

Government
- Issuance of credits
- Registry

Reports issuance of credits

Issues credits

Notifies registration of projects

Government
- Issuance of credits
- Registry

Reports issuance of credits

Issues credits

Request registration of projects

Request issuance of credits

Project Participants

Project Implementation and Monitoring

Project Participants

JCM Projects

Submit PDD for Validation

Submit monitoring report for Verification

Informs results of Validation/ Verification

Third-Party Entity
- Validation and Verification of Projects
- Verifies amount of GHG emissions reduced or removed

GHG = greenhouse gas, JCM = Joint Crediting Mechanism, PDD = project design document.
Source: Adapted from Government of Japan documents.

The roles of individual stakeholders are explained below.

Project Participants. A JCM project typically has two project participants: the main proponent of a JCM project (the project owner in the host country) and a project developer or a technology provider. The project participants prepare and submit a methodology (if required) and the project design document (PDD), implements the JCM project, monitors the project (including GHG emission reductions), and gets the project validated and verified by an accredited third-party entity (TPE). The project participants are accordingly eligible to receive the issued JCM credits.

Joint Committee. The Joint Committee is the governing body for the JCM in a particular host country. It comprises representatives from both the governments of Japan and the host country. It is responsible for, among others, the development of rules and guidelines for the implementation of the JCM, the approval of new methodologies, approval or rejection of proposed methodologies, registration of JCM projects, accreditation of TPEs, approval or rejection of requests for credit issuance, and developing the registries.

Secretariat. The secretariat is established by the Joint Committee to manage the implementation of the JCM in a particular host country. The JCM secretariat services the Joint Committee and relevant stakeholders and is responsible for information dissemination to all parties. This includes publishing documents such as proposed methodologies and PDDs, conducting completeness check of PDDs and Monitoring Reports, and notifying and announcing decisions of the Joint Committee.

Third-party entities. The TPEs are independent auditors designated by the Joint Committee to conduct validation and verification activities under the JCM in a particular host country. TPEs can be existing designated operational entities accredited by the Clean Development Mechanism (CDM) Executive Board, as well as International Organization for Standardization (ISO) 14065 certification bodies.

1.4   RULES AND GUIDELINES

For each host country there is a set of rules and guidelines for the implementation of the JCM (Table 1.1). All stakeholders are required to follow the latest version of the rules and guidelines issued by their respective Joint Committees. While they have been largely identical among all the JCM host countries there are a few exceptions on some details.[2] The latest rules and guidelines, as well as forms and spreadsheets required, are available on the JCM websites of each host country. A list of JCM websites of each host country can be found in Appendix 8.

Table 1.1: Rules and Guidelines for the Joint Crediting Mechanism

Purpose		Rules and Guidelines
Overall		• Rules of Implementation for the Joint Crediting Mechanism • Joint Crediting Mechanism Project Cycle Procedure • Glossary of Terms • Joint Crediting Mechanism Guidelines for Designation as a Third-Party Entity
Joint Committee		• Rules of Procedures for the Joint Committee
Methodology development		• Joint Crediting Mechanism Guidelines for Developing Proposed Methodology
Project procedures	PDD	• Joint Crediting Mechanism Guidelines for Developing Project Design Document and Monitoring Report
	Monitoring	
	Validation	• Joint Crediting Mechanism Guidelines for Validation and Verification
	Verification	

PDD = project design document.
Source: The Joint Crediting Mechanism. Accessed on 15 September 2016 at https://www.jcm.go.jp/

---

[2] For an example, during approval process of a new methodology, additional review process by the secretariat will be required in the case of Indonesia.

1.5 ELIGIBLE PROJECT TYPES

In principle, any GHG reduction activity implemented in a host country and that falls under at least one of the eligible sectors can be developed as a JCM project, as long as it meets the rules and guidelines of the JCM. JCM project types are divided into the following 15 sectors:

(i)   energy industry (renewable and nonrenewable sources),

(ii)   energy distribution,

(iii)   energy demand,

(iv)   manufacturing industries,

(v)   chemical industry,

(vi)   construction,

(vii)   transport,

(viii) mining/mineral production,

(ix)   metal production,

(x)   fugitive emissions from fuel (solid, oil, and gas),

(xi)   fugitive emissions from production and consumption of halocarbons and sulphur hexafluoride,

(xii)   solvent use,

(xiii) waste handling and disposal,

(xiv)   afforestation and reforestation,[3] and

(xv)   agriculture.

All registered projects so far are in the sectors of energy industry (renewable energy) and energy efficiencies under different sectors such as energy demand, manufacturing, and transport. The list of registered projects is in Appendix 1. An updated list can be found on the JCM website.

In addition, there are seven eligible GHGs: carbon dioxide (CO_2), methane (CH_4), nitrous oxide (N_2O), hydrofluorocarbons (HFCs), perfluorocarbons (PFCs), sulphur hexafluoride (SF_6), and nitrogen trifluoride (NF_3). Projects must result in a reduction (or removal) of one of these types of GHGs in order to be eligible.

---

[3]   For Indonesia, this sectoral scope is referred to as "Reducing emissions from deforestation and forest degradation in developing countries; and the role of conservation, sustainable management of forests and enhancement of forest carbon stocks in developing countries (REDD-plus)."

MODULE 2:
DEVELOPMENT OF JOINT CREDITING MECHANISM PROJECTS

2.1 INTRODUCTION TO THE MODULE

Module 2 provides an overview of the development cycle of the Joint Crediting Mechanism (JCM).[4] This module also provides information about support available in developing a JCM project and the approximate costs associated with the various stages. This module is divided into four subsections: (2.1) Introduction to the Module, (2.2) Project Development Cycle, (2.3) Financing Available for the JCM, and (2.4) Costs Associated with the JCM.

2.2 PROJECT DEVELOPMENT CYCLE

Figure 2.1 provides an overview of the JCM project development cycle with the corresponding reference to the module where its detailed explanation is provided. The following subsections provide a brief explanation of each step.

Figure 2.1: Joint Crediting Mechanism Project Development Cycle

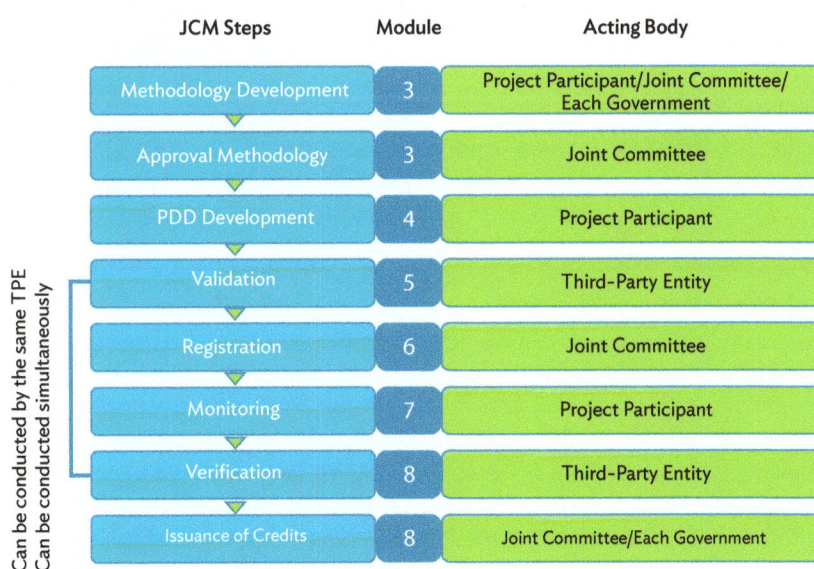

JCM Steps	Module	Acting Body
Methodology Development	3	Project Participant/Joint Committee/Each Government
Approval Methodology	3	Joint Committee
PDD Development	4	Project Participant
Validation	5	Third-Party Entity
Registration	6	Joint Committee
Monitoring	7	Project Participant
Verification	8	Third-Party Entity
Issuance of Credits	8	Joint Committee/Each Government

Can be conducted by the same TPE
Can be conducted simultaneously

JCM = Joint Crediting Mechanism, PDD = project design document.
Source: Adapted from Government of Japan documents.

---

[4] The JCM project cycle is similar to the CDM project cycle. However, the JCM adopts a simpler and more practical approach to carrying out each stage while maintaining the integrity and effectiveness of the mechanism.

2.2.1   Methodology Development

Methodology is defined in the JCM bilateral agreement as "a methodology applied to JCM projects for calculating emission reductions achieved by each project and monitoring the JCM project." A JCM project must use an approved methodology or a combination of approved methodologies in order to be registered as a JCM project. Each approved methodology has specific eligibility criteria. If there is no approved methodology applicable to a proposed JCM project in the particular host country, the project participants will have to develop a new methodology, or propose an amendment to an existing methodology, in order to proceed with the JCM.[5] The process for having a methodology approved is outlined in the next section. Methodology development is discussed in detail under Module 3.

If an applicable methodology is available for the proposed JCM project, project participants can proceed to the project design document (PDD) development.

2.2.2   Approval of Methodology

The project entity submits the proposed methodology to the Joint Committee of the respective host country. The proposed methodology will then undergo a completeness check that takes up to 7 calendar days, followed by a period of 15 calendar days for public inputs. After the public inputs period, the proposed methodology will undergo assessment by the Joint Committee. This takes up to 60 calendar days (in the event that there are clarifications from the Joint Committee, the period could be extended up to 90 calendar days from the closing of public inputs).[6] The methodology approval process is discussed in detail under Module 3.

2.2.3   Project Design Document Development

The project participants prepares the PDD using the latest PDD form available on the JCM website and the monitoring spreadsheet from the approved methodology(ies). The purpose of the PDD is to provide a detailed overview of the proposed JCM project, including:

(i)   a project description,

(ii)   a description of the advanced low-carbon technology used,

(iii)   a list of methodology eligibility conditions and explanation of how the project meet these conditions,

(iv)   estimated emission reductions,

(v)   the proposed monitoring plan, and

(vi)   an assessment of the expected impact of the project on the environment and information regarding local stakeholder consultation.

The PDD is the key document in the JCM development procedure, and the main source of information for the validation, registration, verification of projects, and the issuance of JCM credits. The PDD should also be supplemented by a monitoring plan. The form for the monitoring plan is part of the methodology used. The PDD should follow the *Joint Crediting Mechanism Guidelines for Developing*

---

5   A list of approved methodology can be found in Appendix 2. Updated list is also available on the JCM website of each country.

6   In the case of Indonesia, there is an additional review process by the secretariat after the public inputs period. For the details, please refer to the *Joint Crediting Mechanism Project Cycle Procedure* for Indonesia.

Project Design Document and Monitoring Report, and the applied methodology(ies). PDD development is discussed in detail under Module 4.

2.2.4   Validation

Validation is the independent evaluation of a proposed JCM project by a third-party entity (TPE). Validation assesses the projects' compliance with the JCM requirements in accordance with the *Guidelines for Validation and Verification.*

For each JCM project, a TPE accredited by the host country must be appointed by the project participants. The project participants submit the PDD and the modalities of communication statement (MOC)[7] to the TPE and the secretariat simultanously, to initiate validation. Validation is carried out in line with the *Guidelines for Validation and Verification.* As part of the validation, the TPE also conducts a site visit and interviews local stakeholders, who are the "public, including individuals, groups, or communities affected, or likely to be affected, by the proposed JCM project or actions leading to the implementation of such project, and local governments."[8] A period of 30 calendar days for public inputs is conducted by the secretariat simultaneously with the validation process by making the PDD publicly available through the JCM website. The proceedings of the public input period are noted by the TPE, and are considered during the validation. Based on the assessment and findings of the validation, the TPE prepares a validation report, which is submitted to the project participant.[9] Validation can be conducted simultaneously with verification. Validation is discussed in detail under Module 5.

2.2.5   Registration

Registration is the formal acceptance of a JCM project. Once the project participants receive a positive validation opinion from the TPE, the project participants may proceed to submit their PDD, validation report, MOC, and a completed JCM Project Registration Request Form to the secretariat[10] to officially request registration. Submissions are done electronically. The proposed project will undergo a completeness check within 7 calendar days, and the project participants and the TPE will be notified of the conclusion regarding the completeness of the submission.[11] Upon positive conclusion of the completeness check, the Joint Committee decides if the proposed JCM project will be registered.

When the Joint Committee decides to register the proposed JCM project, the secretariat notifies each side, the project participants, and the TPE of the registration while making the relevant information on the project publicly available through the JCM website. Registration is discussed in detail under Module 6.

---

[7]   MOC identifies the focal point of a JCM project designated to communicate with the secretariat and the Joint Committee on behalf of all of the project participants.

[8]   Defined in the Joint Crediting Mechanism Glossary of Terms of Indonesia under Local Stakeholder consultation

[9]   In the case of Bangladesh, the TPE should submit the validation report to the Joint Committee and project participants.

[10]   In the case of Indonesia, a positively reviewed Sustainable Development Implementation Plan (SDIP) should be submitted as part of the request for registration.

[11]   In the case of Indonesia, there will be an additional review process by the secretariat after the completeness check. For details, please refer to the Joint *Crediting Mechanism Project Cycle Procedure* for Indonesia.

2.2.6　Monitoring

Monitoring is the collection of data and information from the implemented JCM project that is necessary for the calculation of GHG emission reductions in line with the monitoring plan included in the registered PDD. Once a project is implemented, monitoring of the required parameters should be carried out in accordance with the registered PDD.

A monitoring period is the period of time that monitoring takes place for each monitoring report. There are no specific requirements regarding the length of a monitoring period. Project participants can choose the monitoring period based on their own assessment. Once monitoring is completed for a certain monitoring period, the collected data, information, and corresponding calculations for emission reductions are reported through the monitoring report using relevant sections of the registered PDD.[12] The monitoring report is then used as the basis for the verification process and issuance of credits. Monitoring is discussed in detail under Module 7.

2.2.7　Verification

Verification is the independent evaluation of the monitoring report (including data and emission reductions calculation) for a JCM project. It is carried out in line with the *Guidelines for Validation and Verification*. The implemented project is also assessed against the description in the registered PDD and methodology to ensure it complies.[13] A verification report is prepared by the TPE containing the results and findings of the assessment and will be used as a basis for the amount of credits to be issued for the JCM project. During verification, the TPE may also conduct a site visit and interview relevant stakeholders. Verification can be conducted simultaneously with validation and is discussed in detail under Module 8.[14]

Box 1: Considerations in Conducting Validation and Verification Simultaneously

The Joint Crediting Mechanism (JCM) allows validation and verification to be conducted simultaneously by the same third-party entity (TPE). This is one of the key features of the JCM and a difference with the Clean Development Mechanism. This allows project developers to concentrate their efforts on project development and starting operations in the early stages when resources are often stretched, and to handle JCM matters once the operation is on track. There is an added benefit of saving TPE costs. However, it needs to be noted that the project participants are taking both the registration risk and issuance risk by deferring the validation process until after the project is operational. They need to be confident at the beginning of operation that the project meets all JCM requirements so they can subsequently apply to attain registration status.

Source: Authors.

---

[12]   In the case of Indonesia, a sustainable development implementation report (SDIR) should be prepared in line with the positively reviewed SDIP and the *Joint Crediting Mechanism Guidelines for Developing Sustainable Development Implementation Plan and Report for Indonesia.*

[13]   In the event that the project differs from what was described in the registered PDD and/or methodology, proper steps must be taken to address such changes. Details of the procedure is further explained in Module 9.

[14]   In the case of Indonesia, project participants need to submit the monitoring report and SDIR to the Joint Committee at the start of verification for further processing. For details, please refer to the *Joint Crediting Mechanism Project Cycle Procedure* for Indonesia.

2.2.8 Issuance of Credits

JCM credits will be issued based on the results and findings of the verification report. Upon receiving the verification report from the TPE, project participants request issuance of credits by submitting a Credits Issuance Request Form, information on the allocation of credits among the project participants on a prorata basis, the verified monitoring report, and the verification report to the Joint Committee through the secretariat. After conducting the completeness check for 7 calendar days, the Joint Committee decides the amount of credits to be issued based on the verification report. Each government issues the credits to the relevant accounts of the project participants in their respective registries. The secretariat archives all the data of issuance of credits and makes them publicly available through the JCM website. Issuance of credits is discussed in detail under Module 8.

2.3 FINANCING AVAILABLE FOR THE JOINT CREDITING MECHANISM

2.3.1 Introduction

The current bilateral arrangements between Japan and different host countries do not authorize international trading of the JCM credits. Therefore, project participants cannot currently obtain emission reduction revenue by selling JCM credits to overseas buyers, unlike in the Clean Development Mechanism (CDM). While domestic trading of JCM credits may become possible once registries and appropriate national regulations are in place, such systems are yet to be established in JCM host countries.

There are three sources of financial support currently available to JCM projects, as shown in the Table 2.1. They are the Model Project Program and the Demonstration Project Program provided through the Government of Japan, and the Japan Fund for the Joint Crediting Mechanism provided through the Asian Development Bank (ADB).

Table 2.1: Overview of Financing Support for Joint Crediting Mechanism Projects

	Financial Support		Eligible Entity
Government of Japan			
Model Project Program	Subsidy to cover up to 50% of the project's initial investment costs		Japanese entity (as applicant); host country partner also required
Demonstration Project Program	Funding for initial investment cost (partial repayment at a later date)		Japanese entity (as applicant); host country partner also required
Asian Development Bank			
Japan Fund for the Joint Crediting Mechanism	Sovereign project	Grant	ADB borrower
	Nonsovereign project	Interest subsidy for ADB loan	

Source: Authors.

The Government of Japan has also provided funding for JCM feasibility studies since 2010, to source applicable advanced low-carbon technologies, source potential projects, and develop JCM methodologies. Over 400 feasibility studies have been conducted in over 40 countries so far, including 22 from Asia and the Pacific. Most projects under the Model and Demonstration Project

Programs have successfully completed JCM feasibility studies funded by the Government of Japan prior to their selection.

The above sources of financial support for JCM projects are provided during the initial phases of project development and implementation, and can supplement the initial investment cost or mitigate the financing cost of the JCM project. The availability of financing upfront can assist to overcome critical barriers for low-carbon projects, including high upfront investment costs or risks associated with project viability.

2.3.2 Government of Japan

Joint Crediting Mechanism Model Project Program

The JCM Model Project Program was initiated by the Ministry of the Environment of Japan in 2013. The program provides a financial subsidy to project participants to cover up to 50% of the project's initial investment costs. The scope of financing includes facilities and equipment that reduce or avoid GHG emissions as well as construction costs for installing such facilities. Projects that receive the subsidy is chosen through a competitive selection process managed by the Global Environment Centre Foundation (GEC), which functions as a secretariat of the JCM Model Project Program.

The scheme requires an international consortium to be formed between entities of Japan and the host country. The international consortium is required to apply for JCM project registration; conduct monitoring, reporting, and verification (MRV); and deliver at least half of the credits to the Government of Japan when the JCM credits are issued. The Japanese entity within the international consortium is eligible to submit the application and receive the subsidy, and is responsible to the Ministry of the Environment for implementing the project. As such, any host country project developer wishing to avail itself of support under the JCM Model Project Program has to find a partner in Japan.

Subsidy applications are received multiple times a year on an irregular basis. The application evaluation criteria include: project feasibility, projected amount of greenhouse gas (GHG) emission reductions, cost-effectiveness, possibility of technology diffusion, and maturity of JCM methodology, among others. GEC evaluates proposals received and successful applicants are decided in consultation with the Ministry of the Environment.

To date, over 80 JCM Model Projects in Bangladesh, Cambodia, Costa Rica, Ethiopia, Indonesia, Kenya, Malaysia, the Maldives, Mexico, Mongolia, Myanmar, Palau, Saudi Arabia, Thailand, and Viet Nam have been selected. A list containing all JCM Model Projects can be found in Appendix 3. Further information can be found on the JCM website by the GEC.[15]

Joint Crediting Mechanism Demonstration Project Program

The New Energy and Industrial Technology Development Organization (NEDO), an affiliate agency of the Ministry of Economy, Trade and Industry of Japan manages the JCM Demonstration Project Program. This program provides financing to cover part of the initial investment costs associated with implementing advanced low-carbon technologies including the basic design costs, manufacturing cost of equipment and cost of international transport. Financing is also available to cover the costs associated with JCM MRV and the TPE. Similar to the Model Projects, NEDO holds a competitive selection process to determine which projects will receive funding support.

---

[15]   The Joint Crediting Mechanism. Accessed on 15 September 2016 at http://gec.jp/jcm/index.html

Under this scheme, a memorandum of understanding between NEDO and the host country ministry, and an implementation document between the project participants from Japan and the host country are established to formally start the project. A Japanese entity must be engaged, as it is the Japanese project participant that submits the application for support and receives funding from NEDO.

The 'demonstration period' under the program is a maximum of 2 years. Within this period, installation of the equipment and 1 year of operation and monitoring must take place. While MRV is mandatory, unlike the Model Project, issuance and delivery of JCM credits is not required.

The Demonstration Project Program has a unique requirement for project participants to repay part of the equipment cost back to NEDO after a designated period. Its rules stipulate that, during the demonstration period, NEDO has legal ownership of the equipment installed through the program while the host country project participant is allowed to operate it. At the end of the demonstration period, the Japanese project participant is required to buy back the equipment from NEDO and reimburses the equipment cost less depreciation. In practice, the Japanese entity often subsequently sells the equipment to the host county partner. Thus, the scheme allows the host country entity to purchase the equipment at a discounted price after at least 1 year of operating the equipment.

Since the program was launched in Japanese fiscal year 2013, 10 JCM demonstration projects in Indonesia, the Lao People's Democratic Republic (Lao PDR), Mongolia, and Viet Nam have been selected and contracted. A list containing all JCM demonstration projects to date can be found in Appendix 3.

2.3.3   Asian Development Bank

The Japan Fund for the Joint Crediting Mechanism (JFJCM) is an ADB trust fund established in June 2014. It provides financial incentives, in the form of grants and technical assistance, for the adoption of advanced low-carbon technology, to JCM eligible projects that are financed by ADB. Both sovereign and nonsovereign projects are eligible to receive support from the JFJCM.

The Government of Japan has been making annual contributions to the JFJCM and its cumulative support amounts to ¥4.8 billion ($42.6 million equivalent) to date. Further contributions are expected in future years.

The first project to receive support from the JFJCM is a smart microgrid system in the Maldives.

Eligible countries. ADB developing member countries (DMCs) that have signed a JCM bilateral agreement with the Government of Japan are all eligible for support. These DMCs currently include Bangladesh, Cambodia, Indonesia, the Lao PDR, the Maldives, Myanmar, Mongolia, Palau, Thailand, and Viet Nam. Other DMCs will be eligible upon signing a bilateral agreement.

ADB-financed projects. To receive support from the JFJCM, the projects have to be financed by ADB or ADB-administered funds. Projects that are cofinanced by other banks or donors are also eligible, but only the ADB-financed portion is eligible for a grant from the JFJCM.

Advanced low-carbon technologies. Since one of the important objectives of the JFJCM is to promote the use of advanced low-carbon technologies, the project must include the adoption of a technology that reduces GHG emissions. Technologies in any sector are eligible on the condition that they have a proven implementation and operation record of technical effectiveness and GHG emission reduction capacity. The technology also has to include energy-related CO_2 emission reductions. The technology should have a track record but it does not have to be in the host country; it can be in a developed country or another developing country.

Sovereign projects. For sovereign projects, the JFJCM provides support in the form of a grant. The grant can reach up to 10% of the project cost or $10 million, whichever is smaller. For projects that cost less than $50 million, the maximum grant amount is $5 million.

Nonsovereign projects. For projects in which the borrower is in the private sector or the project is not guaranteed by the DMC government, the JFJCM grant is provided as an interest subsidy to reduce the interest payment of the ADB loan. The grant can reach up to 10% of the project cost or $10 million, whichever is smaller.

2.4 COSTS ASSOCIATED WITH THE JOINT CREDITING MECHANISM

The costs associated with the JCM project development cycle involve fees paid to TPEs, and consultants, if such are employed. Unlike the CDM, no fees are required for registration or for issuance of credits. Table 2.2 shows the potential costs associated with the JCM.

Table 2.2: Potential Costs Associated with the Joint Crediting Mechanism Cycle

Item	Payee
Methodology development (if required)	Consultant
Project design document development	Consultant
Validation	Third-party entity
Assistance in validation	Consultant
Monitoring of emission reduction	Consultant/monitoring equipment supplier
Monitoring report preparation	Consultant
Verification	Third-party entity
Assistance in verification	Consultant

Source: Authors.

Third-party entity. The JCM rules require that a TPE conducts validation for project registration and verification for credit issuance. A fee for hiring a TPE is the only cost that a project participant is certain to incur. TPE costs range widely depending on the project type, methodology used, project location, and composition of the auditing team, among other factors. (Refer to Module 5.4 for further information on TPE selection.) The JCM financing programs mentioned in Section 2.3 may support part of the TPE cost, depending on the program requirements.

Consultant. Although it is not a requirement, there are merits in retaining a consultant to assist with the JCM cycle. There are currently few consultants who specialize in the JCM. However, consultants with GHG emission reduction project experience, such as CDM projects, should be able to manage the procedures required under the JCM. Among the different steps in the JCM project development cycle, methodology development is a process that requires a lot of technical skill and expertise. Accordingly, it may give project developers reassurance if the task is outsourced to an experienced consultant, so that time and money are effectively spent at the early stages of project development. The JCM financing programs mentioned in Section 2.3 may support all or part of the cost for consultants or may provide technical assistance for projects.

Monitoring equipment. If additional monitoring equipment, such as loggers or meters, are required specifically for JCM monitoring, the cost for purchasing this equipment will have to be borne by the project participants.

MODULE 3:
METHODOLOGY DEVELOPMENT

3.1 INTRODUCTION TO THE MODULE

Module 3 aims to help project participants to understand the concept and process for developing a new JCM methodology. This module is divided into seven subsections: (3.1) Introduction to the Module, (3.2) Overview of JCM Methodologies, (3.3) Concept of Eligibility Criteria, (3.4) Approach to Calculating Emission Reductions, (3.5) Structure of a Proposed Methodology, (3.6) Methodology Approval Process, and (3.7) Revision of Approved Methodologies.

3.2 OVERVIEW OF METHODOLOGIES

There are currently 25 approved methodologies in different host countries in the categories of energy demand, energy efficiency, and renewable energy. The approved methodologies to date are listed in Appendix 2.[16] An example of an approved methodology is provided in Appendix 4.

Guidelines for developing proposed methodologies are available from the Joint Committee in each host country. Unlike the CDM, methodologies are specific to the host country's context and are approved by the Joint Committee of the respective host country. Understanding the process and the requirements for a host country from the secretariat and the Joint Committee will be critical in developing a methodology. The links to the official JCM websites of each host country are provided in Appendix 8.

3.3 CONCEPT OF ELIGIBILITY CRITERIA

Each JCM methodology must contain specific eligibility criteria that determine whether a proposed project is eligible under the methodology. The eligibility criteria should be able to be objectively examined and confirmed during validation. Therefore, eligibility criteria that need to be monitored ex post should be avoided.

Eligibility criteria cover the following two requirements:

    (a) conditions for the project to be registered as a JCM project, and
    (b) conditions for the project to be able to apply the JCM methodology.

---

[16] The updated list of approved methodologies are available on the JCM websites of each host country.

Examples of eligibility criteria for (a) include the type of technology and product specifications, such as minimum design efficiency (e.g., output per kilowatt-hour [kWh]) or preapproved advanced low-carbon technology, product types (e.g., air conditioners with inverters, electric vehicles, or photovoltaic-battery combinations). Examples of eligibility criteria for (b) include the availability of data needed to calculate emission reductions, such as the availability of historical data and reference emissions.

Table 3.1 provides an example of how eligibility criteria are defined in a JCM methodology using approved methodology VN_AM002, *Introduction of Room Air Conditioners Equipped with Inverters.*

Table 3.1: Eligibility Criteria under Approved Methodology VN_AM002, *Introduction of Room Air Conditioners Equipped with Inverters*

No.	Description as per the Methodology	Explanation
Criterion 1	The methodology is applicable to the following types of projects: – Installation of inverter room air conditioners (RACs) to public sector buildings – Replacement of existing non-inverter RACs by inverter RACs in all types of buildings	Eligibility criteria (a) and (b) Indicates the applicable technology (inverter RAC), location (public sector buildings), and pre-project situation (used non-inverter RACs, which will be replaced by the new inverter RAC)
Criterion 2	Rated cooling capacity of a project RAC is within the applicable range of the Vietnamese national standard TCVN7831:2012	Eligibility criteria (a) and (b) Indicates the technical specification and the performance level of the measure to be implemented.
Criterion 3	Ozone depletion potential (ODP) of the refrigerant used for project RAC is zero	Eligibility criteria (b) This criterion was set to ensure that there is no potential release of ozone-depleting refrigerants from the project.
Criterion 4	Plans to prevent release of refrigerants into the atmosphere at the time of RAC removal are prepared for both project RACs and the existing RACs replaced by the project. In the case of replacing existing RACs by project RACs, execution of the prevention plan is checked at the time of verification, in order to confirm that refrigerant used for the existing RACs removed by the project is not released into the air.	Eligibility criteria (b) Refrigerants used in RACs normally have ozone-depleting or greenhouse effects. The criterion ensures proper handling of the refrigerants from the replaced RACs.

Source: The Joint Crediting Mechanism. Methodology : VN_AM002 Ver1.0. Accessed on 15 September 2016 at https://www.jcm.go.jp/vn-jp/methodologies/16

3.4 APPROACH TO CALCULATING EMISSION REDUCTIONS

Under the JCM, emission reductions are calculated as the difference between reference emissions and project emissions.

According to the *Joint Crediting Mechanism Glossary of Terms*, reference emissions should be below business-as-usual (BAU) emissions.[17] The reference emissions represent a conservative estimate of

---

[17]   As defined in the glossary of terms, "BAU emissions represent plausible emissions in providing the same outputs or service level of the proposed JCM project in the host country."

what would occur without the JCM project. Project emissions refer to the actual amount of GHGs emitted once the project has been implemented.

To ensure that JCM methodologies are conservative, project participants must use either: (i) conservative reference emissions, or (ii) conservative project emissions. In some cases, both (i) and (ii) may be applied.

3.4.1   Setting Conservative Reference Emissions

In JCM methodologies, the reference emissions are set lower than the BAU emissions to ensure that the methodology is conservative.

The reference scenario and reference emissions are set considering the following types of factors:

(i)   the current situation and performance,

(ii)   the average historical performance,

(iii)   performance of similar products and technologies that compete with the project technology,

(iv)   legal requirements, and

(v)   best available technology.

For example, in case of introducing a new advanced low-carbon technology from overseas, the BAU may be based on historical data, and the reference emissions may be set based on the best available technology in the host country which is still less efficient than the proposed project. The process described here is conceptual, and it is up to the methodology proponent to provide justification in setting the reference emissions. Figure 3.1 shows a graphical representation of how setting the reference emissions lower than BAU emissions results in a conservative calculation of emission reductions.

Figure 3.1: Calculation of Emission Reductions Using Reference Emissions

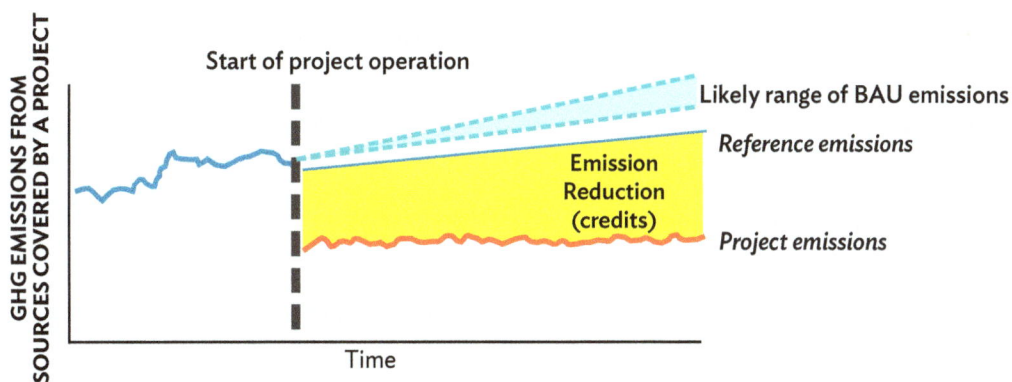

BAU = business-as-usual, GHG = greenhouse gas.

Source: Adapted from Government of Japan documents.

> **Box 2: Example of Setting Reference Scenario in Approved Methodology**
> **ID_AM003, *Installation of Energy-Efficient Refrigerators Using Natural Refrigerant at Food Industry Cold Storage and Frozen Food Processing Plant***
>
> This methodology applies to projects in the food industry and aims to reduce electricity consumption by using high-efficiency refrigerators using natural refrigerant.
>
> The reference scenario is the case wherein the project uses reference refrigerators with its coefficient of performance (COP) derived conservatively from the maximum value available among the possible types of refrigerators. The reference emissions are calculated by multiplying the amount of electricity consumption of the project refrigerator with the ratio of the COPs of the project and reference refrigerators, and the CO_2 emission factor for consumed electricity.
>
> $$RE_p = \sum_i \left\{ EC_{PJ,i,p} \times (COP_{PJ,i} \div COP_{RE,i}) \times EF_{elec} \right\}$$
>
> | | | |
> |---|---|---|
> | RE_p | : | Reference emissions during the period p [tCO_2/p] |
> | $EC_{PJ,i,p}$ | : | Amount of electricity consumption of the project refrigerator i during the period p [MWh/p] |
> | $COP_{PJ,i}$ | : | COP of the project refrigerator type i |
> | $COP_{RE,i}$ | : | COP of the reference refrigerator type i |
> | EF_{elec} | : | CO_2 emission factor for consumed electricity [tCO_2/MWh] |
>
> The COP of common refrigerators (as in the business-as-usual scenario) is in the range of 1.60–1.65, which has been collected from the manufacturers with high market share in Indonesia. The example project set the COP for its reference scenario at 1.7, which indicates that the reference emissions were calculated conservatively.
>
> MWh = megawatt-hour, tCO_2 = tons of carbon dioxide.
> Source: The Joint Crediting Mechanism. Methodology : ID_AM003 Ver2.0. Accessed on 15 September 2016 at https://www.jcm.go.jp/id-jp/methodologies/26

3.4.2   Setting Conservative Project Emissions

Project emissions refer to emissions resulting from the implementation of the JCM project. Project emissions are normally calculated using monitored data (post implementation) or conservatively set default values. The methodology proponent may choose to use conservative default values that will result in calculated project emissions that are larger than the actual project emissions.[18] Using default values reduces the burden of monitoring and simplifies verification at a later stage. Figure 3.2 shows a graphical representation of how using default values for the calculation of project emissions results in conservative calculation of emission reductions.

---

[18]   The conservativeness of the default value must be justified by the methodology proponent and will be assessed during the methodology approval process.

Figure 3.2: Calculation of Emission Reductions Using Conservative Project Emissions

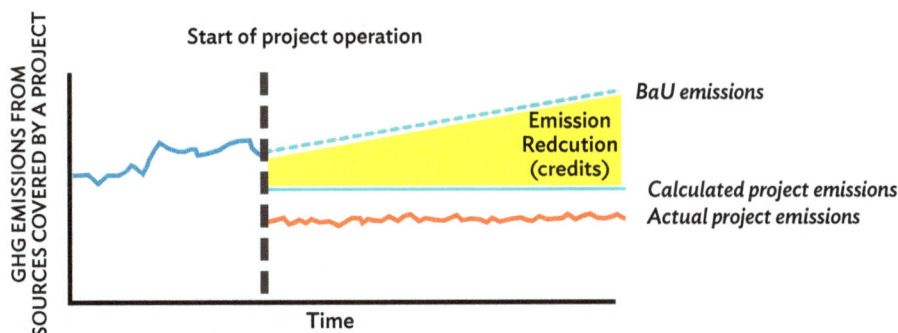

BAU = business-as-usual, GHG = greenhouse gas.

Source: Adapted from Government of Japan documents.

3.5 STRUCTURE OF A PROPOSED METHODOLOGY

Methodology proponents who wish to propose a JCM methodology must submit a proposal to the JCM Secretariat consisting of the following documents:

(i)   Proposed Methodology Form, and

(ii)   Proposed Methodology Spreadsheet.

The *Joint Crediting Mechanism Guidelines for Developing Proposed Methodology* contains instructions on how to develop a methodology, which are available on the JCM website of each host country.

3.5.1   Proposed Methodology Form

The *Proposed Methodology Form* contains all of the details of the proposed methodology. It follows the same form as that of an approved methodology. The information that must be provided is listed in this section using the example of the Approved Methodology VN_AM002: *Introduction of room air conditioners equipped with inverters*.[19]

---

[19]   The Joint Crediting Mechanism. Methodology : VN_AM002 Ver1.0. Accessed on 15 September 2016 at https://www.jcm.go.jp/vn-jp/methodologies/16

Title of the Methodology

The title of the proposed methodology should

(i)   reflect the project types to which the methodology is applicable, but not be project-specific;

(ii)   include the GHG emission reduction measures, such as technology; and

(iii)   indicate the version number of the document.

Figure 3.3: Section A of VN_AM002: *Introduction of room air conditioners equipped with inverters*

A. Title of the methodology

Introduction of room air conditioners equipped with inverters, Version 01.0

Source: The Joint Crediting Mechanism. Methodology : VN_AM002 Ver1.0. Accessed on 15 September 2016 at https://www.jcm.go.jp/vn-jp/methodologies/16

Terms and Definitions

The terms that are used in the proposed methodology need to be clearly defined and used consistently.

Figure 3.4: Section B of VN_AM002

B. Terms and definitions

Terms	Definitions
Room air conditioner (RAC)	A single split type air conditioner.
Inverter	A device included in RACs and other motor-operated appliances, whose function is to vary the speed of the compressor motor in line with different load demand, for example to enable variable refrigerant flow to optimally regulate the temperature.
Public sector buildings	Buildings owned or administered by national or local government.
Energy efficiency ratio (EER)	The ratio of total cooling capacity to rated input power in specified conditions.
Cooling seasonal performance factor (CSPF)	Energy efficiency of RACs factoring into the seasonal temperature variation. Ratio of the total annual amount of heat that the RAC can remove from the indoor air when operated for cooling active mode to the total annual amount of energy consumed by the equipment during the same period.

Source: The Joint Crediting Mechanism. Methodology : VN_AM002 Ver1.0. Accessed on 15 September 2016 at https://www.jcm.go.jp/vn-jp/methodologies/16

Summary of the Methodology

This section contains a summary of four key elements of the methodology, as specified in the methodology form.

Figure 3.5: Section C of VN_AM002

C. Summary of the methodology	
Terms	**Definitions**
GHG emission reduction measures	Energy saving achieved by introduction of RACs equipped with inverters.
Calculation of reference emissions	GHG emissions associated with electricity consumption of reference RACs are calculated based on the monitored electricity consumption of project RACs, the ratio of the energy efficiency of reference and project RACs, and the CO_2 emission factor of the electricity consumed by project RACs.
Calculation of project emissions	GHG emissions associated with electricity consumption of project RACs are calculated based on the monitored electricity consumption of project RACs and the CO_2 emission factor of the electricity consumed by project RACs.
Monitoring parameters	Electricity consumption of project RACs. Project energy efficiency (CSPF of project RACs). Reference energy efficiency (CSPF of reference RACs).

CO_2 = carbon dioxide, CSPF = cooling seasonal performance factor, GHG = greenhouse gas, RAC = room air conditioner.

Source: The Joint Crediting Mechanism. Methodology : VN_AM002 Ver1.0. Accessed on 15 September 2016 at https://www.jcm.go.jp/vn-jp/methodologies/16

Eligibility Criteria

The eligibility criteria describe how the methodology is applicable to the specific project. This is a key component of the methodology. According to the *JCM Guidelines for Developing Proposed Methodology*, eligibility criteria should have the following characteristics:

(i)   Eligibility criteria are those that can be examined objectively.

(ii)   Eligibility criteria include
   • characteristics to identify the measures (e.g., technology, product, or service) applied to the methodology, and
   • conditions that are necessary to enable robust calculation of GHG emission reductions by the algorithm contained in the methodology (e.g., the situation before the implementation of the measure, in cases where reference emissions are calculated on the basis of historical performance of the facility).

(iii)   Eligibility criteria should, to the extent possible, be those that can be ascertained upon validation; i.e., eligibility criteria should avoid those that need to be monitored ex post. For example, actual performance of a measure should not be included as an eligibility criterion, since it is not certain at the validation whether the stated performance can be achieved. On the other hand, performance as defined by nameplate figures can be included as an eligibility criterion since it can be readily checked upon validation.

(iv)   Eligibility criteria may be represented by
- a certain technology (e.g., ultra supercritical coal-fired power plants),
- a certain technology with a design efficiency or performance indicator above a certain threshold (e.g., a power plant with a thermal efficiency above X%), or
- a certain sector to which the measure is applied.

Figure 3.6: Section D of VN_AM002

D. Eligibility criteria	
This methodology is applicable to projects that satisfy all of the following criteria:	
Criterion 1	The methodology is applicable to the following types of projects: • Installation of inverter RACs to public sector buildings. • Replacement of existing non-inverter RACs by inverter RACs in all types of buildings.
Criterion 2	Rated cooling capacity of a project RAC is within the applicable range of the Vietnamese national standard TCVN7831:2012.
Criterion 3	Ozone Depletion Potential (ODP) of the refrigerant used for project RAC is zero.
Criterion 4	Plans to prevent release of refrigerants into the atmosphere at the time of RAC removal are prepared for both project RACs and the existing RACs replaced by the project. In the case of replacing existing RACs by project RACs, execution of the prevention plan is checked at the time of verification, in order to confirm that refrigerant used for the existing RACs removed by the project is not released to the air.

RAC = room air conditioner.

Source: The Joint Crediting Mechanism. Methodology : VN_AM002 Ver1.0. Accessed on 15 September 2016 at https://www.jcm.go.jp/vn-jp/methodologies/16

Emission Sources and Greenhouse Gas Types

This section should provide a complete list of all GHG emissions by source that are significant and reasonably attributable to the JCM project in both the reference scenario and the project scenario. All GHG types and emission sources should be included[20] for example, CO_2 for fossil fuel consumption by the facility, or CH_4 for methane emission from waste. This section should also include justification for excluding any sources related to the reference emissions or the project emissions. Upstream emissions may be excluded unless they are deemed significant.

---

[20]   In case the emissions of a particular GHG type are negligible they can be omitted with justification.

Figure 3.7: Section E of VN_AM002

E. Emission Sources and GHG types	

Reference emissions	
Emission sources	GHG types
Electricity consumption by reference RACs	CO_2
Project emissions	
Emission sources	GHG types
Electricity consumption by project RACs	CO_2

CO_2 = carbon dioxide, GHG = greenhouse gas, RAC = room air conditioner.

Source: The Joint Crediting Mechanism. Methodology : VN_AM002 Ver1.0. Accessed on 15 September 2016 at https://www.jcm.go.jp/vn-jp/methodologies/16

Establishment and Calculation of Reference Emissions

As explained above, reference emissions are the estimated emissions that would have occurred under the reference scenario. The *JCM Guidelines for Developing Proposed Methodology* prescribes the following guidelines for establishing reference emissions:

(i)   Only one procedure for establishing reference emissions should be provided.

(ii)   This, in the view of the methodology proponent, should represent the plausible emissions that would occur in providing the same outputs or service level that will be provided by the proposed JCM project in the host country.

(iii) Reference emissions should be established, taking into account the following:
- If the reference emissions are defined by multiplying an emission factor and an output, the output should be identical to or less than the monitored output of the project.
- The reference emissions should comply with all applicable regulations of the host country.

(iv)   A description on how the reference emissions are derived should be provided, together with a description of how and why the reference emissions are below BAU emissions.

(v)   Reference emissions may be derived from
- the current situation and performance,
- average historical performance,
- performance of similar products and technologies that compete with the project technology,
- legal requirements,
- voluntary standards and targets, or
- best available technology of the host country.

(vi)   The method to calculate reference emissions should be elaborated in a way that is specific and complete enough so that the procedure could be carried out in an unambiguous way, replicated, and subjected to assessment and verification. The following should be taken into account:

- The underlying rationale for the method to calculate should be explained (e.g., marginal vs. average, etc.).
- Consistent variables, equation formats, subscripts, etc. should be used.
- All equations in the Proposed Methodology Form should be numbered.
- All variables, with units indicated, should be defined.
- Conservativeness of the method of calculation should be justified.

(vii) All parameters, coefficients, and variables used in the calculation of reference emissions should be explained:
- For those values that are provided in the methodology,
  ° precise references from which these values are taken should be clearly indicated (e.g., official statistics, Intergovernmental Panel on Climate Change [IPCC] guidelines, commercial and scientific literature), and
  ° conservativeness of the values provided should be justified.
- For those values that are to be provided by the project participants, it should be clearly indicated how the values are to be selected and justified, for example, by explaining the following:
  ° what types of sources are suitable (official statistics, expert judgment, proprietary data, IPCC guidelines, commercial and scientific literature, etc.),
  ° the vintage of data that is suitable,
  ° what spatial level of data is suitable (local, regional, national, international), and
  ° how conservativeness of the values is to be ensured.

(viii) For all data to be monitored or recorded by the project participants, the procedures to be followed if expected data are unavailable should be specified. For instance, the methodology could point to a preferred data source, and indicate a priority order for use of additional data and/or fallback data sources to preferred sources (e.g., private, international statistics, etc.).

(ix) Any parameters, coefficients, variables, etc. that are used to calculate reference emissions that are obtained through monitoring should be noted.

(x) Any parts of the method to calculate that are not self-evident should be explained. Provide references as necessary. Explain implicit and explicit key assumptions in a transparent manner.

(xi) When referring to and/or making use of life cycle analysis (LCA) and/or LCA tools, methodology proponents should provide, in a transparent manner, all equations, parameterizations, and assumptions used in the LCA. For example, this could be accomplished by highlighting the relevant sections in an attached copy of the referenced LCA.

(xii) The most recent IPCC default values may be used when country- or project-specific data are not available or difficult to obtain.

(xiii) Methodologies requiring sampling as a part of monitoring should clearly indicate the sampling method and statistical treatment of sampled data (e.g., confidence level, margin of error). A useful reference is the statistical treatment of sampled data for large-scale CDM project activities in the latest version of the *Standard: Sampling and surveys for CDM project activities and programmes of activities*.

(xiv) Emission reductions from reduced consumption of international transport fuels cannot be claimed under the JCM.

Figure 3.8: Section F of VN_AM002

F. Establishment and calculation of reference emissions

F.1. Establishment of reference emissions

Reference emissions are established as the product of monitored electricity consumption of project RACs, the ratio of the energy efficiency of reference and project RACs, and the CO_2 emission factor of the electricity consumed by project RACs.

The methodology provides following stepwise procedures to set energy efficiency values of the reference and project RACs, ex-post. In the procedures, reference RACs are conservatively set to results in a net reduction of emissions.

Step 1: Determine reference RACs that lead to net emission reduction
Select a reference RAC for each model of project RAC which meets the following conditions:
- Not equipped with inverters.
- Categorized as Grade 4 of the energy efficiency grades by EER as outlined in Table 3 of Vietnamese national standard TCVN7830:2012.
- Cooling capacity of the reference RAC selected for the purpose of calculating reference emissions belongs to the same rated capacity class as the project RAC, based on the three rated capacity classes in Table 3 of TCVN7830:2012.
- Reference RAC is previously unused and is currently available in the market at the time of CSPF determination.

Step 2: Determine CSPF of reference RACs
CSPF values of selected reference RACs by step 1 are determined at a third-party testing facility which is equipped with a calorimeter capable of determining CSPF in line with ISO5151, following the testing procedures and conditions outlined in the latest version of Vietnamese National Standard TCVN 7831 at the time of CSPF determination.

Step 3: Determine CSPF of project RACs
CSPF values of each model type of project RACs are determined at a third party testing facility which is equipped with a calorimeter capable of determining CSPF in line with ISO5151, following the testing procedures and conditions outlined in the latest version of Vietnamese National Standard TCVN 7831 at the time of CSPF determination.

Step 4: Select the reference and project energy efficiency (CSPF) values for the project
Among the CSPF values calculated in Step 2 and 3, select the highest value of CSPF determined according to step 2 and the lowest value of CSPF determined according to step 3 to yield the efficiency ratio (η_{PJ} / η_{REF} in equation 1). These values are used as the reference and project CSPF values during the project lifetime. This step ensures that ratio of CSPF values used for the purpose of calculating reference emissions is conservatively derived for the project.

continued on next page

Figure 3.8 *continued*

F.1. Establishment of reference emissions

$$RE_p = \sum_{i=1}^{n} EC_{PJ,i,p} \times \left(\frac{\eta_{PJ}}{\eta_{REF}}\right) \times EF_{elec} \qquad (1)$$

Where

RE_p	=	Reference emissions during the period p [tCO$_2$/p]
$EC_{PJ,i,p}$	=	Electricity consumption by project RACs group i during the period p [MWh/p]
n	=	Number of RACs groups whose aggregate electricity consumption are measured by one electricity meter [dimensionless]
i	=	An index variable that is used to count the number of RACs groups
η_{REF}	=	Highest energy efficiency (CSPF) of reference RACs[1] [dimensionless]
η_{PJ}	=	Lowest energy efficiency (CSPF) of project RACs[2] [dimensionless]
EF_{elec}	=	CO$_2$ emission factor of electricity consumed [tCO$_2$/MWh]

CSPF = cooling seasonal performance factor, EER = energy efficiency ratio, MWh = megawatt-hour, RAC = room air conditioner, tCO$_2$ = tons of carbon dioxide.

[1] CSPF of the reference RAC selected using steps as stipulated in Section F.1.
[2] CSPF of the project RAC selected using steps as stipulated in Section F.1.

Source: The Joint Crediting Mechanism. Methodology : VN_AM002 Ver1.0. Accessed on 15 September 2016 at https://www.jcm.go.jp/vn-jp/methodologies/16

Calculation of Project Emissions

In this section, the method and steps to calculate the project emissions should be described. It should closely follow the methods and steps proposed to calculate the reference emissions, where possible. (For the concept of project emissions, refer to Section 3.4.)

Figure 3.9: Section G of VN_AM002

G. Calculation of project emissions

$$PE_p = \sum_{i=l}^{n} EC_{PJ,i,p} \times EF_{elec} \qquad (2)$$

Where

PE_p	=	Project emissions during the period p [tCO$_2$/p]
$EC_{PJ,i,p}$	=	Electricity consumption by project RACs group i during the period p [MWh/p]
EF_{elec}	=	CO$_2$ emission factor of electricity consumed [tCO$_2$/MWh]

CO$_2$ = carbon dioxide, MWh = megawatt-hour, RAC = room air conditioner, tCO$_2$ = tons of carbon dioxide.
Source: The Joint Crediting Mechanism. Methodology : VN_AM002 Ver1.0. Accessed on 15 September 2016 at https://www.jcm.go.jp/vn-jp/methodologies/16

Calculation of Emission Reductions

In this section, the method to calculate emission reductions should be described. Emission reductions are the difference between reference emissions and project emissions.

Figure 3.10: Section H of VN_AM002

H. Calculation of emissions reductions

$$ER_p = RE_p - PE_p \qquad (3)$$

Where

ER_p	=	Emission reductions during the period p [tCO$_2$/p]
RE_p	=	Reference emissions during the period p [tCO$_2$/p]
PE_p	=	Project emissions during the period p [tCO$_2$/p]

tCO$_2$ = tons of carbon dioxide.

Source: The Joint Crediting Mechanism. Methodology : VN_AM002 Ver1.0. Accessed on 15 September 2016 at https://www.jcm.go.jp/vn-jp/methodologies/16

Data and Parameters Fixed ex ante

Data and parameters under this section are fixed at the time of validation (ex ante) and monitoring is not required. For simplicity of the emission reduction calculation and validation process, conservatively set default values are often applied. All default values used in the methodology shall be listed with their sources properly identified.

Figure 3.11: Section I of VN_AM002

I. Data and parameters fixed *ex ante*

Parameter	Description of data	Source
EF_{elec}	CO$_2$ emission factor of electricity consumed. When captive power generation is not available at the project site, then the most recent Vietnamese national grid emission factor [EF$_{grid}$] available at the time of validation is applied as [EF$_{elec}$] and fixed for the monitoring period thereafter.	[EF$_{grid}$] Ministry of Natural Resources and Environment of Vietnam (MONRE), Vietnamese DNA for CDM unless otherwise instructed by the Joint Committee.

continued on next page

Figure 3.11 *continued*

	When captive power generation is available at the project site, then [EF_{elec}] is conservatively selected as below and fixed for the monitoring period thereafter: $$EF_{elec} = \min(EF_{grid}, EF_{captive})$$ $$EF_{captive} = 0.8 \text{ tCO}_2/\text{MWh}^*$$ *The most recent emission factor available from CDM approved small scale methodology AMS-I.A at the time of validation is applied.	[$EF_{captive}$] CDM approved small scale methodology: AMS-I.A
n	Number of RACs groups whose aggregate electricity consumption are measured by one electricity meter [dimensionless]	The project proponent selects an integer between 1 and 25 in line with the number of RACs groups included in the project.

CDM = Clean Development Mechanism, CO_2 = carbon dioxide, DNA = designated national authority, MWh = megawatt-hour, RAC = room airconditioner, tCO_2 = tons of carbon dioxide.

Source: The Joint Crediting Mechanism. Methodology : VN_AM002 Ver1.0. Accessed on 15 September 2016 at https://www.jcm.go.jp/vn-jp/methodologies/16

3.5.2   Proposed Methodology Spreadsheet

The proposed methodology spreadsheet (PMS) must be prepared by the methodology proponents to accompany the proposed methodology form. It is a critical document as it presents the emission reductions calculation process for a particular methodology, and serves as the basis for the monitoring spreadsheet. The PMS consists of an input sheet and a calculation process sheet.

The monitoring spreadsheet forms part of an approved methodology. It consists of a monitoring plan sheet, monitoring structure sheet, and monitoring report sheet. The input sheet and calculation process sheet are developed from the PMS. Figure 3.12 shows the structure of the monitoring spreadsheet.

Figure 3.12: Structure of the Monitoring Spreadsheet

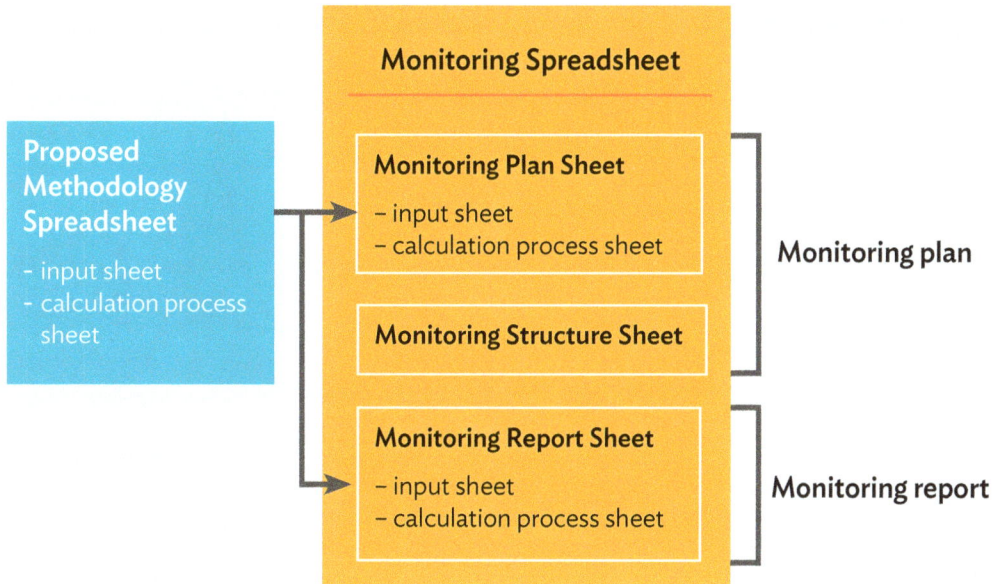

Source: Authors.

After the PMS is prepared by the methodology proponent and the methodology is approved by the Joint Committee, the secretariat will convert the PMS into the monitoring plan sheet and monition report sheet, with minor editorial changes. The monitoring structure sheet will be prepared and added by the secretariat to complete the monitoring spreadsheet.

Only the PMS is required to be prepared by the methodology proponent. However, this section explains the requirements of the monitoring spreadsheet, not the PMS, as the monitoring spreadsheet is based off the PMS, and is the final form of the spreadsheet of an approved methodology.

The monitoring spreadsheet comprises the following worksheets:

(i)   Monitoring plan sheet (input sheet and calculation process sheet), which is used for developing a monitoring plan and calculating emission reductions ex ante;

(ii)   Monitoring structure sheet, which is used for developing an operational and management structure to be implemented during monitoring; and

(iii) Monitoring report sheet (input sheet and calculation process sheet), which is used for developing a monitoring report and calculating emission reductions ex post.

The details of each worksheet, as labelled under the monitoring spreadsheet, are provided below. Figures used under this section provide examples of actual worksheets taken from Approved Methodology VN_AM003: *Improving the energy efficiency of commercial buildings by utilization of high efficiency equipment.*[21]

---

[21]   The Joint Crediting Mechanism. Methodology : VN_AM003 Ver1.0. Accessed on 15 September 2016 at https://www.jcm.go.jp/vn-jp/methodologies/17

Monitoring Plan Sheet (Input Sheet)

The first part of the monitoring plan sheet is its input worksheet (MPS [input]), which identifies and describes each parameter necessary for the calculation of emission reductions. The values entered in this MPS (input) worksheet subsequently refer to the adjacent calculation process sheet. The parameters contained in this worksheet provide a complete list of the data that needs to be collected for the application of the methodology, and the methodology proponent needs to make sure that they are in line with relevant sections in the proposed methodology form. In this worksheet, a list of parameters to be monitored ex post is described and provided in its Table 1 (Figure 3.13); project-specific parameters to be fixed ex ante in its Table 2 (Figure 3.14); and the ex ante estimation of GHG emission reductions in its Table 3 (Figure 3.15).

For parameters to be monitored ex post (Table 1), the required inputs from the methodology proponents are as follows:

- Parameter: The variable used in equations in the proposed methodology;
- Description of data: A clear and unambiguous description of the parameter;
- Estimated values: This may be left blank at the methodology proposal stage, as it is for the project participants to fill in for the calculation of emission reductions;
- Unit: The International System Unit[22] is to be used;
- Monitoring options: Selected from the options below. If more than one option is used, provide the order of priority and the conditions:

  Option A: based on public data that is measured by entities other than the project participants (data used: publicly recognized data such as statistical data and specifications);

  Option B: based on the amount of the transaction that is measured directly using measuring equipment (data used: commercial evidence such as invoices);

  Option C: based on the actual measurement using measuring equipment (data used: measured values);

- Source of data: Description of which data sources should be used to determine this parameter. How the values are to be selected and justified has to be clearly indicated, for example, the types of data sources (e.g., official statistics, expert judgment, proprietary data, IPCC, commercial and scientific literature, logbooks, daily records, surveys) and spatial level of data (e.g., local, regional, national, international);
- Measurement methods and procedures: For options B and C, provide a description of the measurement procedures or reference to appropriate standards, including quality assurance and quality control (QA/QC) procedures;
- Monitoring frequency: Describe the monitoring frequency (e.g., continuously, annually).

---

[22] Bureau Internationale des Poids et Mesures. Measurement units: the SI. Accessed on 15 September 2016 at http://www.bipm.org/en/measurement-units/

Figure 3.13: Monitoring Plan Sheet (Input Sheet) Worksheet, Table 1 of VN_AM003: *Installation of Energy-Efficient Refrigerators Using Natural Refrigerant at Food Industry Cold Storage and Frozen Food Processing Plant*

Table 1: Parameters to be monitored ex post

(a) Monitoring point No.	(b) Parameters	(c) Description of data	(d) Estimated Values	(e) Units	(f) Monitoring option	(g) Source of data	(h) Measurement methods and procedures	(i) Monitoring frequency	(j) Other comments
1	$FC_{PJ1,i,p}$	Fossil fuel consumed during the period p by the high efficiency equipment i introduced in the project categorized as measure 1		L/p	Option C	Monitored data	Fossil fuel consumption is monitored by a volumetric meter subject to maintenance/calibration/replacement in line with manufacturer's or meter suppliers' specifications	Monitored continuously and recorded monthly	
2	$EC_{PJ2,i,p}$	Electricity consumed during the period p by the high efficiency equipment i introduced in the project categorized as measure 2		kWh/p	Option C	Monitored data	Electricity consumption is measured by an electricity meter. The meter is calibrated or replaced in line with relevant national/international standards, or manufacturer's specifications.	Monitored continuously and recorded monthly	
3	t_p	Operating hours of auxiliary electric equipment during the period p		hr/p	Option C	Monitored data	Operating hours are checked against an operation record taken by the project participant	monitored and recorded monthly	
4	$t_{i,p}$	Operating hours of the high efficiency equipment i introduced in the project during the period p categorized as measure 3		hr/p	Option C	Monitored data	Operating hours are checked against an operation schedule prepared by the project participant.	monitored and recorded monthly	

hr = hour, kWh = kilowatt-hour.

Source: The Joint Crediting Mechanism. Methodology : VN_AM003 Ver1.0. Accessed on 15 September 2016 at https://www.jcm.go.jp/vn-jp/ methodologies/17

Parameters that are to be fixed ex ante (Table 2) should also adhere to the instructions provided for parameters to be monitored ex post where applicable, and should be considered under "I. Data and parameters fixed ex ante" as described in Section 3.5.1.

Figure 3.14: Monitoring Plan Sheet (Input Sheet) Worksheet, Table 2 of VN_AM003

Table 2: Project-specific parameters to be fixed ex ante

(a) Parameters	(b) Description of data	(c) Estimated Values	(d) Units	(e) Source of data	(f) Other comments
$\eta_{PJ1,i}$	Energy efficiency of the equipment i introduced in the project		dimensionless	Rated/provided by the technology supplier	
$\eta_{REF1,i}$	Energy efficiency of the reference equipment replaced/substituted by the equipment i introduced in the project		dimensionless	Default values are applied - New natural gas fired boiler (w/o condenser): 92% - New oil fired boiler: 90% - New coal fired boiler: 85% The latest version of CDM Tool to determine the baseline efficiency of thermal or electric energy generation systems	
ECR_i	Rated electricity consumption of the high efficiency equipment i introduced in the project		kW	Rated/provided by the technology supplier	
H_i	Rated heating capacity of the high efficiency equipment i introduced in the project		kW	Rated/provided by the technology supplier	
DC_i	Unit fuel consumption rate of the reference equipment replaced/substituted by the equipment i introduced in the project		L/kWh	Rated/provided by the technology supplier	
CH_i	Rated cooling capacity of the high efficiency equipment i introduced in the project		kW	Rated/provided by the technology supplier	
COP_i	Efficiency of the reference equipment replaced/substituted by the equipment i introduced in the project		dimensionless	Default values are applied Cooling Capacity/unit (USRT) - x ≤ 250 USRT: COP 5.71 - 250 USRT < x ≤ 300 USRT: COP 5.75 - 300 USRT<x ≤ 500 USRT: COP 5.91	
$ECR_{REF3,i}$	Rated electricity consumption of the reference equipment i replaced by the high efficiency equipment i in the project categorized as measure 3		kW	Rated/provided by the technology supplier	
ECA	Capacity of auxiliary electric equipment that is installed due to the implementation of the high efficiency equipment i		kW	Rated/provided by the technology supplier	
$EC_{PJ3,i}$	Rated electricity consumption of the high efficiency lighting i in the project categorized as measure 3		kW	Rated/provided by the technology supplier	

continued on next page

Figure 3.14 *continued*

$EC_{PJ3,i}$	Rated electricity consumption of the high efficiency lighting i in the project categorized as measure 3	kW	Rated/provided by the technology supplier
$EF_{CO2,ELEC}$	CO_2 emission factor of the electricity consumed When captive power generation is not available at the project site, then the most recent Vietnamese national grid emission factor [EF_{grid}] available at the time of validation is applied as [$EF_{CO2,ELEC}$] and fixed for the monitoring period thereafter. When captive power generation is available at the project site, then [$EF_{CO2,ELEC}$] is conservatively selected as below and fixed for the monitoring period thereafter: $EF_{CO2,ELEC}$ = min (EF_{grid}, $EF_{captive}$) $EF_{captive}$ = 0.8 tCO_2/MWh* *The most recent emission factor available from CDM approved small scale methodology AMS-I.A at the time of validation is applied.	tCO_2/MWh	[EF_{grid}] Ministry of Natural Resources and Environment (MONRE), Vietnamese DNA for CDM unless otherwise instructed by the Joint Committee. [$EF_{captive}$] CDM approved small scale methodology: AMS-I.A
EF_{CO2}	CO_2 emission factor of fossil fuel	tCO_2/L	Country specific data or IPCC default value from "2006 IPCC Guidelines for National Greenhouse Gas Inventories". Lower limit values of the default net calorific value and CO_2 emission factor are applied.

CDM = Clean Development Mechanism, kW = kilowatt, L/kWh = liter per kilowatt-hour, MWh = megawatt-hour, tCO_2 = tons of carbon dioxide.

Source: The Joint Crediting Mechanism. Methodology: VN_AM003 Ver1.0. Accessed on 15 September 2016 at https://www.jcm.go.jp/vn-jp/ methodologies/17

Figure 3.15: Monitoring Plan Sheet (Input Sheet) Worksheet, Table 3 of VN_AM003

Table3: *Ex-ante* **estimation of CO_2 emission reductions**

CO_2 emission reductions	Units
#DIV/0!	tCO_2/p

[Monitoring option]

Option A	Based on public data which is measured by entities other than the project participants (Data used: publicly recognized data such as statistical data and specifications)
Option B	Based on the amount of transaction which is measured directly using measuring equipments (Data used: commercial evidence such as invoices)
Option C	Based on the actual measurement using measuring equipments (Data used: measured values)

tCO_2/p = tons of carbon dioxide during the period p.

Source: The Joint Crediting Mechanism. Methodology : VN_AM003 Ver1.0. Accessed on 15 September 2016 at https://www.jcm.go.jp/vn-jp/ methodologies/17

Monitoring Plan Sheet (Calculation Process Sheet)

The second part of the monitoring plan sheet is the calculation process worksheet (MPS[cal_process]). The purpose of this worksheet is to calculate the reference emissions, project emissions, and the resulting emission reductions. A list of all of the default values that cannot be changed by the project participants should be provided. When all of the parameters are entered into the MPS(input) sheet, the MPS(calc_process) worksheet should calculate the reference emissions, project emissions, and emission reductions to be automatically.

Figure 3.16 shows excerpts of the main sections of the MPS(calc_process) worksheet. Default values in this example include efficiencies of the reference and project boilers, and the coefficient of performance of the reference chiller.

Figure 3.16: Monitoring Plan Sheet (Calculation Process Sheet) Worksheet of VN_AM003

	Fuel type	Value	Units	Parameter
1. Calculations for emission reductions				
Emission reductions during the period p	N/A	#DIV/0!	tCO_2/p	ER_p
2. Selected default values, etc.				
Efficiency of reference boiler		0.00	-	$\eta_{REF1,i}$
Efficiency of project boiler		0.00	-	$\eta_{PJ1,i}$
COP of reference chiller		0.00	-	COP_i
3. Calculations for reference emissions				
Reference emissions during the period p	N/A	#DIV/0!	tCO_2/p	RE_p
Reference emissions (Fuel consumption)		#DIV/0!	tCO_2/p	-
Fossil fuel consumed during the period p by reference equipment (measures 1 and 2)		#DIV/0!	L/p	$\Sigma FC_{REF,i,p}$
Fossil fuel consumed during the period p by the reference equipment (measure 1)		#DIV/0!	L/p	$FC_{REF,1,p}$
4. Calculations of the project emissions				
Project emissions during the period of p	N/A	0.0	tCO_2/p	PE_p
Project emissions (Fuel consumption)		0.0	tCO_2/p	-
Fossil fuel consumed during the period p by the high efficiency equipment (measure 1)		0	L/p	$FC_{PJ1,i,p}$
CO_2 emission factor of fossil fuel		0.00000	tCO_2/L	EF_{CO2}
Project emissions (Power consumption)		0.0	tCO_2/p	-
Total electricity consumed during the period p by the high efficiency equipment (measure 2 and 3)	Electricity	0	kWh/p	$\Sigma EC_{PJ,i,p}$
Total electricity consumed during the period p by the high efficiency equipment (measure 2)	Electricity	0	kWh/p	$EC_{PJ,2,p}$
Capacity of auxiliary electric equipment		0	kW	ECA_i
Operating hours of auxiliary electric equipment during the period p		0	hr/p	t_p

Figure 3.16 *continued*

[List of Default Values]

Boiler efficiency (new natural gas fired boiler w/o condenser)	0.92	--
Boiler efficiency (new oil fired boiler)	0.90	--
Boiler efficiency (new coal fired boiler)	0.85	--
Chiller COP (x ≤ 250USRT)	5.71	--
Chiller COP (250< x ≤300USRT)	5.75	--
Chiller COP (300 < x ≤500USRT)	5.91	--

hr = hour, kWh = kWh = kilowatt-hour, L = liter, tCO_2 = tons of carbon dioxide.

Source: The Joint Crediting Mechanism. Methodology : VN_AM003 Ver1.0. Accessed on 15 September 2016 at https://www.jcm. go.jp/vn-jp/ methodologies/17

Monitoring Structure Sheet

The monitoring structure sheet provides details on the roles and responsibilities of the personnel who will be monitoring the project. The monitoring structure sheet will be prepared by the secretariat. It will then be completed by the project participants at a later stage when identifying the monitoring structure of a proposed JCM project.

Figure 3.17: Monitoring Structure Sheet of VN_AM003

Monitoring Structure Sheet [Attachment to Project Design Document]

Responsible personnel	Role

Source: The Joint Crediting Mechanism. Methodology : VN_AM003 Ver1.0. Accessed on 15 September 2016 at https://www.jcm. go.jp/vn-jp/ methodologies/17

Monitoring Report Sheet

The input worksheet and calculation worksheet of the monitoring report sheet (MRS [input] and MRS [calc_process]) serve as the template for preparing a monitoring report. The monitoring report is the key document during verification. The contents of these sheets are the taken from the PMS sheets.

The MRS will also be prepared by the secretariat based on the PMS. Once the proposed methodology is approved, the methodology spreadsheet containing the monitoring plan sheet, monitoring structure sheet, and monitoring report sheet should complement the Approved Methodology document. These documents can be found on the websites of each of the host countries (Appendix 8).

Additional Information

This section is not obligatory, but provides an opportunity for the methodology proponent to provide additional information in order to clarify to the Joint Committee, among others, the details of the technology used, justification of the application of the formula presented in the proposed methodology, and/or how the methodology proponent chose the default values conservatively.

Table 3.2 presents some examples of different types of additional information given with the proposed methodology.

Table 3.2: Example of Additional Information Documents

Methodology	Type of Additional Information
VN_AM003: Improving the energy efficiency of commercial buildings by utilization of high efficiency equipment	The methodology proponent has provided additional information to demonstrate that the choice of default values used were conservative. Justification includes that the default values were obtained from the Clean Development Mechanism tool, through a sector survey and market survey, and by selecting the more conservative of the existing values and default values.
ID_AM007: Greenhouse gas emission reductions through optimization of boiler operation in Indonesia	The methodology proponent explains in detail how to obtain the historical specific emission factor of steam through linear regression analysis of 1-year data (taken hourly) before implementation of the project. The methodology proponent also justifies why this method is appropriate. Moreover, the additional information also provides justifications on how the methodology is developed to ensure its conservativeness.

Sources: The Joint Crediting Mechanism. Methodology : VN_AM003 Ver1.0. Accessed on 15 September 2016 at https://www.jcm.go.jp/vn-jp/ methodologies/17; and The Joint Crediting Mechanism. Methodology : ID_AM007 Ver1.0. Accessed on 15 September 2016 at https://www.jcm.go.jp/id-jp/methodologies/12

3.6 METHODOLOGY APPROVAL PROCESS

After preparing the *Proposed Methodology Form* and the accompanying PMS, along with any additional information needed, the methodology proponent should submit all documents to the secretariat. The secretariat will do a completeness check on the proposed methodology. If the submission is considered incomplete by the secretariat, the methodology proponent may revise and resubmit the proposed methodology.

After a successful completeness check, the proposed methodology will be published on the JCM website of the host country for 15 days public inputs.[23] The Joint Committee will assess the proposed methodology based on the submitted materials and submitted public inputs (if any).

During the assessment, the Joint Committee may ask the methodology proponent for clarification, revision, or discussion on the proposed methodology. The methodology proponent should be ready to answer all requests and revise the methodology accordingly. Once the proposed methodology is approved, the secretariat will notify the methodology proponent and publish the documents as an approved methodology on the JCM website. The description of steps is provided in Figure 3.18.

---

[23]   In the case of Indonesia, there is an additional review process by the secretariat after the public input period. For details, please refer to the *Joint Crediting Mechanism Project Cycle Procedure* for Indonesia.

Figure 3.18: Flowchart of the Methodology Approval Process

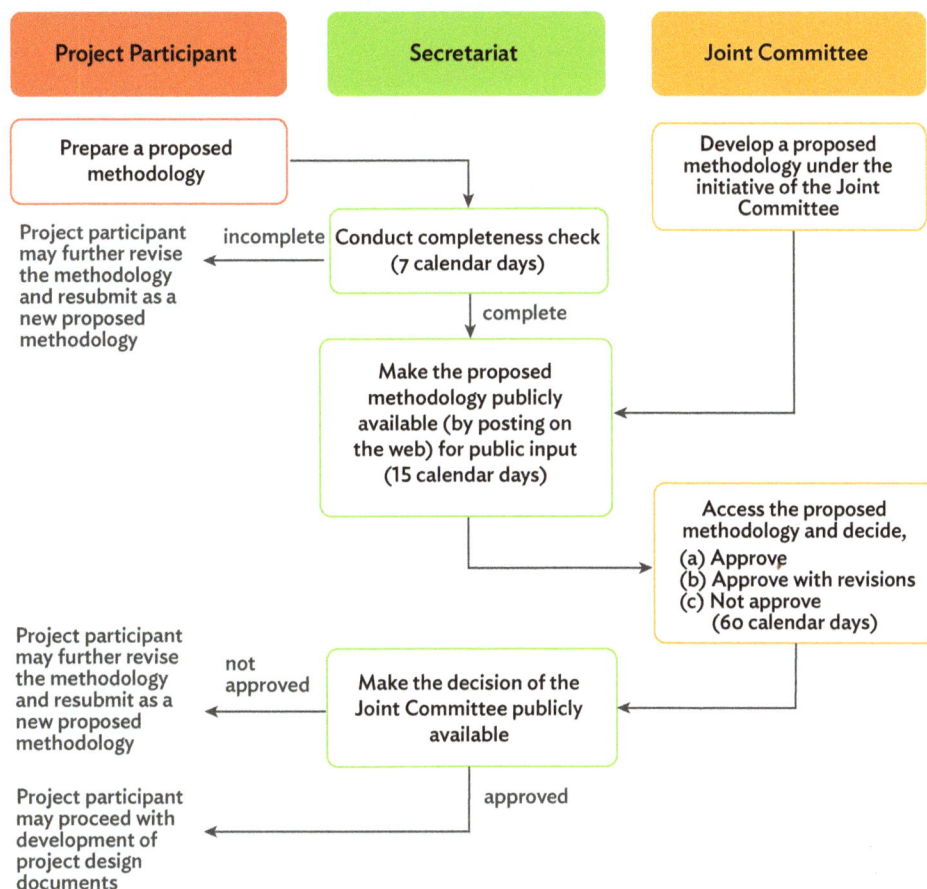

Project Participant	Secretariat	Joint Committee

Prepare a proposed methodology

Develop a proposed methodology under the initiative of the Joint Committee

Project participant may further revise the methodology and resubmit as a new proposed methodology ← incomplete — **Conduct completeness check (7 calendar days)**

complete

Make the proposed methodology publicly available (by posting on the web) for public input (15 calendar days)

Access the proposed methodology and decide,
(a) Approve
(b) Approve with revisions
(c) Not approve
(60 calendar days)

Project participant may further revise the methodology and resubmit as a new proposed methodology ← not approved — **Make the decision of the Joint Committee publicly available**

Project participant may proceed with development of project design documents ← approved

Source: Authors.

The time required for the methodology approval process depends on several factors, such as the complexity of the proposed methodology or the number of issues raised by the Joint Committee. Therefore, it is not possible to generalize the timeline of the approval process. However, all approved methodologies have obtained approval in less than 8 months from the time the proposed methodologies were published for public inputs, and a number of them were approved in 1–2 months.

3.7   REVISION OF APPROVED METHODOLOGIES

Revisions to an approved methodology may be required and carried out in the following cases, among others:

–   new or a better understanding of scientific evidence indicates that emission reductions may be overestimated or underestimated based on the existing approved methodology or that the reductions may not be real, measurable, and verifiable;

- the applicability conditions require broadening to include more potential project types or conditions for use;
- there are identified inconsistencies, errors, and/or ambiguities in the language and/or formulas used within or between methodologies;
- in response to issues raised during the validation process;
- the proposed project is similar to the project anticipated under the existing methodology and only minor revisions are required.

Methodologies may also be revised at the request of the Joint Committee.

The request for revision of an approved methodology is done by submitting the completed JCM Approved Methodology Revision Request Form and the proposed revised methodology highlighting all proposed changes to the secretariat. The submission may be accompanied by additional documents that help explain the proposed revision. The Joint Committee may request the methodology proponents to submit additional documents including a draft project design document (PDD) to which the proposed revised methodology is applied.

The secretariat conducts a completeness check using the same procedure described in Section 3.6. In parallel, the secretariat also assesses the nature and complexity of the proposed revision and classifies it as follows:

(i)   Substantive revision proposal: Substantive changes to the approved methodology including changes in eligibility criteria, calculations, monitoring methods, and parameters; or

(ii)   Editorial revision proposal: Correction of misstatements and editorial revisions to improve the clarity of the approved methodology.

Proposals for revision under classification (i) are subject to public inputs and will follow the same approval procedure described in Section 3.6. Proposals for revision under classification (ii) are reflected as appropriate by the secretariat after approval by the Joint Committee. The secretariat makes the revised methodology publicly available through the JCM website.

Project participants may apply the approved revised methodology to projects seeking validation after the approval date of the revised version. The revision of an approved methodology has no effect on projects that have started the public inputs for draft PDDs applying the previous version of the revised methodology.

MODULE 4:
PROJECT DESIGN DOCUMENT

4.1 INTRODUCTION TO THE MODULE

Module 4 discusses the project design document (PDD) in detail. It outlines the PDD structure, contents, and procedures to assist project participants in developing a comprehensive PDD. This module also provides advice for project participants to prepare a PDD before entering validation with some examples and additional tips. This module is divided into six subsections: (4.1) Introduction to the Module, (4.2) Development of Project Design Document, (4.3) Project Description, (4.4) Application of an Approved Methodology and Calculation of Emission Reductions, (4.5) Environmental Impact Assessment and Local Stakeholder Consultation, and (4.6) Monitoring Plan.

4.2 DEVELOPMENT OF THE PROJECT DESIGN DOCUMENT

The PDD is the main project document in the Joint Crediting Mechanism (JCM) process.[24] The PDD contains all of the necessary information regarding a proposed JCM project and will be the basis for the registration and issuance of credits. The PDD is prepared by the project participants in accordance with the *Guidelines for Developing Project Design Document and Monitoring Report* set up by the Joint Committee of the respective host country. An example of a PDD of a registered project is provided in Appendix 5.

A PDD submission consists of a completed PDD form and a monitoring plan using the monitoring spreadsheet of the approved methodology applied. The PDD form and monitoring spreadsheet can be obtained electronically from the JCM website of the respective host country and should not be altered. The latest version of the PDD form and monitoring spreadsheet of the applied methodology(ies) are required. It is also important that the PDD is accurate, complete, and provides a clear understanding of the proposed JCM project. All documents must be completed in English.

The PDD form includes the following elements:

(i)   Project description, which provides information on the general description of the project and the applied technologies and/or measures and other specific details regarding the project.

(ii)   Application of approved methodology, which provides identifying the specific approved methodology used for the project and describing how the project meets the eligibility criteria of the methodology.

(iii) Emission reduction calculations, where all emission sources are identified and emission reductions are calculated. The section also provides all monitoring points for measurement.

---

[24]   For projects in Indonesia, in addition to the PDD, a sustainable development implementation plan (SDIP) shall be prepared in accordance with the *Joint Crediting Mechanism Guidelines for Developing Sustainable Development Implementation Plan and Report for Indonesia*.

(iv)   Environmental impact assessment, where the potential impacts of the project to the community and environment are analyzed.

(v)   Local stakeholder consultation, where the summary of proceedings from consultation with relevant stakeholders is provided and how their concerns are addressed.

(vi)   References, where relevant supporting documents on the project or the project's emission reductions are provided such as reports, data on laboratory analysis, and national regulations.

The monitoring plan consists of the monitoring plan sheet and the monitoring structure sheet:

(i)   The monitoring plan sheet consists of two sections, the input sheet and the calculation process sheet. Project participants input estimated values for each parameter in the monitoring plan sheet including those fixed ex ante for parameters not to be monitored.

(ii)   The monitoring structure sheet describes the operational and management structure to be implemented in order to conduct monitoring.

It is advisable to consider monitoring issues while developing the PDD to reduce potential issues at a later stage, such as post-registration project changes. Project participants developing a PDD should carefully review Module 7: Monitoring and Reporting and consider the issues mentioned. It should also be noted that the monitoring spreadsheet may be revised when the corresponding approved methodology is revised.

4.3   PROJECT DESCRIPTION

The first section of the PDD contains a short description of the JCM project including how the project contributes to the reduction of greenhouse gas (GHG) emissions. The project description should include the following information:

(i)   title of the project, where the applied technology(ies) and sector that the project is implemented in should be mentioned;

(ii)   general description of how the proposed project reduces GHG emissions, what kind of technology is used, and how the technology will be transferred;

(iii)   detailed location of the project: country; region, state, or province; city, town, or community; latitude and longitude;

(iv)   profile of project participants from Japan and the host country;

(v)   duration of the project with information related to project starting date[25] and operational lifetime;[26] and

(vi)   contribution of the project from Japan to the host country in terms of finance, technology transfer, capacity building, economy, and the community.

Project description has to be accurate, complete, and provide a clear understanding of the JCM project. Figure 4.1 shows an excerpt of a project description from an actual registered JCM project in Indonesia, ID002: *Project of Introducing High Efficiency Refrigerator to a Food Industry Cold Storage in Indonesia*.[27]

---

[25]   The operation starting date of the proposed JCM project should be the starting date indicated in DD/MM/YYY. This will be further confirmed during the validation site visit.

[26]   Should be explained with publicly available statistical data, reference data from similar projects, legal durable year, expert judgment, etc.

[27]   The Joint Crediting Mechanism. Project : ID 002 Project of Introducing High Efficiency Refrigerator to a Food Industry Cold Storage in Indonesia. Accessed on 15 September 2016 at https://www.jcm.go.jp/id-jp/projects/2

Figure 4.1: Project Description Section of ID002: *Project of Introducing High Efficiency Refrigerator to a Food Industry Cold Storage in Indonesia*

The proposed Joint Crediting Mechanism project aims to save energy by introducing a high efficiency refrigerator to a food industry cold storage in Indonesia. The project is expected to reduce 140 tCO_2e of GHG emissions annually through installation of a refrigerator in a newly established food industry cold storage of PT. Adib Global Food Supplies in West Java Province, Indonesia.

In line with the Approved Methodology ID_AM003, reference emissions are calculated by multiplying electricity consumption of the project refrigerator (MWh), ratio of COPs (Coefficient of Performance) for reference/project refrigerators and CO_2 emission factor for electricity consumed (tCO_2e/MWh), while project emissions are calculated by multiplying electricity consumption of the project refrigerator (MWh) and CO_2 emission factor for electricity consumed (tCO_2e/MWh).

COP of the project refrigerator (COP_{PJ}) is 2.2 which is calculated by dividing cooling capacity (189 kW*) of the refrigerator by its electricity consumption (86kW*) based on the manufacturer's catalogue. COP of reference refrigerator (COP_{RE}) is set as 1.71 which is the maximum value among the collected data for commercially available refrigerators in Indonesia to ensure a net emission reduction. Electricity consumption of the project refrigerator will be obtained by monitoring.

The estimated amount of annual electricity consumption by the project refrigerator is 603 MWh, while that of the reference refrigerator is 776 MWh, resulting in 22% of energy saving. The reference emissions are 631 tCO_2e and the project emissions are 491 tCO_2e resulting in an estimated annual GHG emission reduction of 140 tCO_2e.

CO_2 = carbon dioxide, kW = kilowatt, tCO_2e = tons of carbon dioxide equivalent.

* Temperature condition: − 25 °C, Cooling water fed to condenser: inlet 32 °C.

Source: The Joint Crediting Mechanism. Project : ID 002 Project of Introducing High Efficiency Refrigerator to a Food Industry Cold Storage in Indonesia. Accessed on 15 September 2016 at https://www.jcm.go.jp/id-jp/projects/2

Box 3: How to Treat Confidential Information on a Project Design Document

A project design document (PDD) may have confidential information or data, and a project participant may wish to treat such information or data as confidential or proprietary. In this case, the project participant is required to submit documentation in two versions:

- One version of the PDD where all parts containing confidential or proprietary information are covered (e.g., by covering those parts with black ink or overwriting those parts with letters such as "XXX") so that the version can be made publicly available without displaying confidential or proprietary information.

- A second version of the PDD containing all information, which is to be treated as strictly confidential by parties handling this documentation including the third-party entities, the Joint Committee members, and external experts.

Note: The descriptions related to application of the eligibility criteria and the environmental impact assessment are not considered confidential or proprietary.

Source: Guidelines for Developing Project Design Document and Monitoring Report.

4.4 APPLICATION OF AN APPROVED METHODOLOGY AND CALCULATION OF EMISSION REDUCTIONS

4.4.1 Methodology Selection

A JCM project activity must use the most updated version of the methodology that has been approved by the county's Joint Committee. The correct title and version should be quoted and applied in the PDD. Module 3 provides information on how a methodology is developed and the necessary steps for methodology development and approval process.

An example of an application of an approved methodology section from a registered JCM project is provided in Figure 4.2 using MN002: *Centralization of Heat Supply System by Installation of High-Efficiency Heat Only Boilers in Bornuur Soum Project.*[28] There are two subsections: (i) the applied approved methodology and (ii) explanation of eligibility criteria where the project participant needs to demonstrate that the project meets the eligibility criteria specified in the approved methodology.

Figure 4.2: Application of an Approved Methodology Section of MN002: *Centralization of Heat Supply System by Installation of High-Efficiency Heat Only Boilers in Bornuur Soum Project*

B.1. Selection of methodology(ies)

Selected approved methodology no. MN_AM002

Version number: Ver 1.0

B.2. Explanation of how the project meets eligibility criteria of the approved methodology

Eligibility Criteria	Description Specified in the Methodology	Project Information
Criterion 1	Technology to be employed in this methodology is coal-fired heat only boiler (HOB) for hot water supply system	The purpose of the boilers is to heat school, hospital, kindergarten and cultural centre and local governor's office and etc. The boilers are hot water low pressure automatic boilers and designed for brown coal (5–25 mm) burning only.
Criterion 2	Capacity of the project HOB ranges from 0.10MW to 1.00MW	Three high-efficiency coal-fired boilers "EKOEFEKT 600" with capacity of 650 kW each installed at project site.
Criterion 3	The project activity involves the installation of new HOB and/or the replacement of the existing coal-fired HOB	The three new high efficient HOBs "EKOEFEKT 600" of capacity 650 kW each will replace 7 old small inefficient boilers.

continued on next page

[28]   The Joint Crediting Mechanism. Project : MN002 Centralization of heat supply system by installation of high-efficiency Heat Only Boilers in Bornuur soum Project. Accessed 15 September 2016 at https://www.jcm.go.jp/mn-jp/projects/6

Figure 4.2 *continued*

Eligibility Criteria	Description Specified in the Methodology	Project Information
Criterion 4	The project HOB is equipped with an operation and maintenance manual	The manual of boiler operation is prepared in Mongolian language. The maintenance manual of "EKOEFEKT 600" is prepared in Mongolian language.
Criterion 5	The catalog value of the boiler efficiency for the project HOB is 80% or higher	The boiler efficiency of "EKOEFEKT 600" is over 80%, according to the catalog value.
Criterion 6	The project HOB has the function to feed coal on the stoker uniformly and is equipped with a dust collector	The "EKOEFEKT 600" is designed to burn the fuel well and with maximum efficiency. The principle of the boiler's function is to burn, on the cylindrical rotary grate, a controlled supply of fuel under controlled combustion air input. The "EKOEFEKT 600" are designed with separate dust collector.

Source: The Joint Crediting Mechanism. Project : MN 002 Centralization of heat supply system by installation of high-efficiency Heat Only Boilers in Bornuur soum Project. Accessed 15 September 2016 at https://www.jcm.go.jp/mn-jp/projects/6

As seen in the example in Figure 4.2, the project participants must demonstrate how the proposed project meets each of the eligibility criteria for the specific methodology. If the proposed JCM project does not meet all of the eligibility criteria for an approved methodology, the project participant needs to develop a new methodology and have it approved. Alternatively, the project participant can propose a revision to an existing approved methodology. If the project uses more than one methodology, all of the applied approved methodologies have to be listed in the PDD.

Project participants also need to ensure that the project is using the latest version of the approved methodology when the project is submitted for validation. If an updated version of the methodology has been published at the time of the request for registration, project participants may only submit a request using the previous version of the methodology within the grace period of 8 months from the date of publication of the revised methodology.

After the approved methodology is chosen, project participants should identify all emission sources and types of GHGs included in the calculation of reference and project emissions.

Box 4: How to Select from the Available Approved Methodologies

Project participants need to take into account the following points during the methodology selection process:

- Is the methodology approved in the country where the proposed Joint Crediting Mechanism (JCM) project is located?
- Is the methodology the latest version?
- Does the proposed JCM project satisfy all the eligibility criteria on the approved methodology?
- Can the proposed JCM project satisfy all the monitoring requirements of the methodology?

Source: Authors.

4.4.2 Calculation of Emission Reduction

Under the Calculation of Emission Reduction section, project participants shall ensure that all of the relevant GHG emission sources covered in the methodology are addressed in the calculation of project emissions and reference emissions.[29] Eligible GHGs under the JCM are carbon dioxide (CO_2), methane (CH_4), nitrous oxide (N_2O), hydrofluorocarbons (HFCs), perfluorocarbons (PFCs), sulphur hexafluoride (SF_6), and nitrogen trifluoride (NF_3). If the project involves more than one GHG emissions either in the reference emission or project emission, a separate table is to be provided for each component or each approved methodology that is applied. If the approved methodology allows project participants to choose whether a source or GHG is to be included, the project participants may have to reasonably justify that choice using supporting documents.

Figure 4.3 is an example taken from the same registered project from Mongolia. CO_2 is the identified GHG type for the reference and project emissions as shown in its section C.1. The project participants should indicate all emission sources and monitoring points for the project activity. The project participants may wish to add some diagrams or pictures to clearly illustrate the monitoring points as this can be crucial in describing how the project is monitored. This will also be helpful during the validation and verification activities of the third-party entity.

Figure 4.3: Calculation of Emission Reduction Section of MN002

C.1. All emission sources and their associated greenhouse gases relevant to the JCM project

Reference Emissions	
Emission Sources	**GHG Type**
Coal consumption of reference HOB	CO_2
Project Emissions	
Emission Sources	**GHG Type**
Coal consumption of project HOB	CO_2
Electricity consumption of project HOB	CO_2

continued on next page

---

[29] Some methodologies allow project participants to choose certain GHGs to be included or excluded. Justification of the decision will be assessed during the validation.

continued on next page

C.2. Figure of all emission sources and monitoring points relevant to the JCM project

The emission sources are coal consumptions and electrical consumptions in HOB. The monitoring equipment is the heat meter which measures the quantity of net heat supply of HOB. "Monitoring point 1" is the "Heat Quantity" ("PHp") of the heat meter. The "Heat Quantity" is calculated by the flow rate of outgoing heat water/returning heat water ("V1"), the temperature of outgoing heating water ("T1"), and the temperature of returning heating water ("T2").

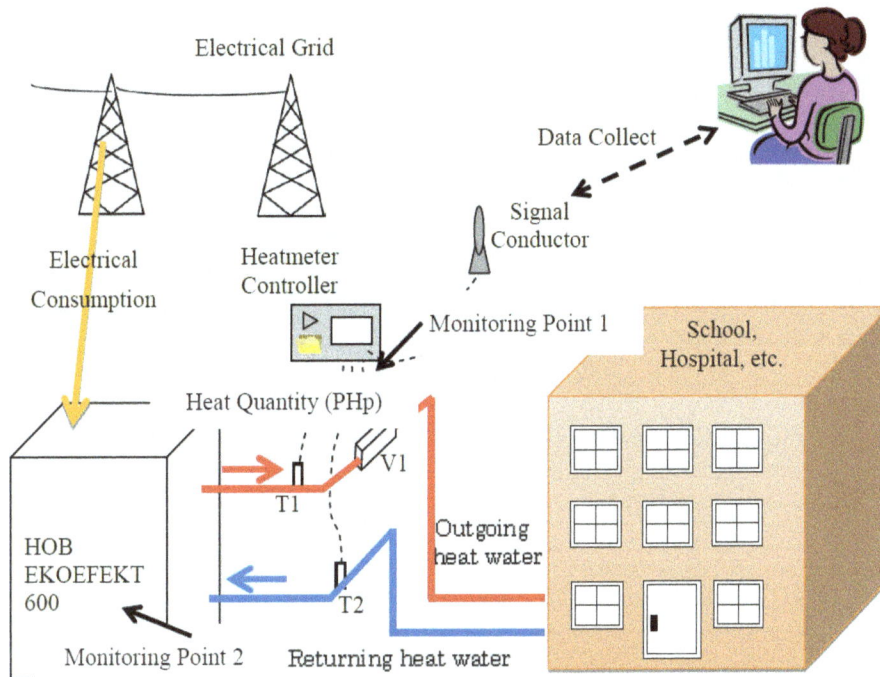

CO$_2$ = carbon dioxide, GHG = greenhouse gas, HOB = heat only boiler, JCM = Joint Crediting Mechanism.

Source: The Joint Crediting Mechanism. Project : MN 002 Centralization of heat supply system by installation of high-efficiency Heat Only Boilers in Bornuur soum Project. Accessed 15 September 2016 at https://www.jcm.go.jp/mn-jp/projects/6

Under section C.3 of the PDD, each JCM project must indicate a year-on-year ex ante GHG emission reduction estimate. Emission reduction calculations (including reference emissions and project emissions), applied values, and assumptions are taken from the applied methodology(ies). In the event that the proposed project has more than one component, an aggregated GHG emission reduction estimation should be provided in this section, whereas a breakdown should be given in the annex of the PDD.

4.5   ENVIRONMENTAL IMPACT ASSESSMENT AND LOCAL STAKEHOLDER CONSULTATION

4.5.1   Environmental Impact Assessment

Project participants are required to indicate in the PDD if an environmental impact assessment (EIA) is a legal requirement for the proposed project. Based on national or local regulations, a project activity may or may not require an EIA. If an EIA is not required, the project participants can indicate this in the PDD and continue with the project. If an EIA is required, the project participants must report on the conclusions of the EIA in the PDD.

4.5.2   Local Stakeholder Consultation

Local stakeholder consultation is also a requirement for JCM projects. The purpose of stakeholder consultation is to inform local stakeholders[30] of the proposed JCM project, solicit comments from them, and address any concerns they may have regarding the project. In addition, the preparation process for conducting the local stakeholder consultations should also be taken into account, such as the communications used to invite and inform local stakeholders of the plan to conduct the consultation. The invitation has to be made in advance to ensure availability of local stakeholders to participate.

The local stakeholders to be consulted will depend on the nature of the project. These can include national and/or local government authorities, heads of communities, local residents, nongovernment organizations, consultants, and other related local stakeholders.

The local stakeholder consultation is usually a half-day to 1 day event led by the project participants. It typically starts with a session to introduce the proposed JCM project and its activities followed by a Question and Answer session where the project participants can answer any concerns or questions that local stakeholders may have. It is important for the project participants to explain the possible effects that the proposed JCM project may have on the stakeholders, especially on the local communities. Any comments received from local stakeholders during the consultation need to be recorded. A summary of these comments must be included in the PDD together with an explanation of the actions taken to address the comments received.[31]

A stakeholder consultation conducted under an EIA may be recognized as a JCM local stakeholder consultation in certain JCM host countries such as Indonesia. In such a case, a separate consultation process specifically for the JCM project is not necessary.

---

[30]   According to the Joint Crediting Mechanism Glossary of Terms of Indonesia, local stakeholders implies "public, including individuals, groups or communities affected, or likely to be affected, by the proposed JCM project or actions leading to the implementation of such project, and local governments."

[31]   These will be reviewed by TPE during the validation site visit.

4.6 MONITORING PLAN

The monitoring plan of a JCM project is prepared using the monitoring plan sheet and monitoring structure sheet of the monitoring spreadsheet included in the latest approved methodology applied for the proposed project. The monitoring plan is included as an attachment to the PDD rather than allotted a specific section within the PDD.

4.6.1 Monitoring Plan Sheet

The monitoring plan sheet consists of two sections, the input worksheet (MPS [input]), and the calculation process worksheet (MPS [calc_process]). Project participants input estimated values for each parameter in the MPS(input), including those fixed ex ante for parameters not to be monitored.[32] For each parameter, the project participant is required to specify the following in line with the applied methodology:

- Estimated values: Provide an estimated value for the parameter for the purpose of calculating emission reductions of the proposed project ex ante;

- Monitoring options: Select an option from options A to C, if such option is available:

  Option A: based on public data that is measured by entities other than the project participants (data used: publicly recognized data such as statistical data and specifications);

  Option B: based on the amount of transaction that is measured directly using measuring equipment (data used: commercial evidence such as invoices);

  Option C: based on the actual measurement using measuring equipment (data used: measured values);

- Source of data, measurement methods and procedures, monitoring frequency: detailed information specific to the proposed project may be added in line with the applied methodology.

Box 5: Selecting the Monitoring Option

Project participants are required to select monitoring option(s) for each parameter, where Option A allows the use of public data, such as official statistics for monitoring, and Option B accepts the use of transaction data, such as commercial evidence. Actual measurement using measuring equipment is required for Option C.

In many cases, methods under Options A and B are less burdensome for project participants to monitor, as Option C requires the use of measurement equipment, which may only be used for JCM monitoring. Such equipment is required to be calibrated in accordance with the laws and regulations of the host country, or in line with international standards or manufacturers' specification. At the same time, Option C may allow a more accurate measurement of the project, enable counting of more emission reductions.

Source: Authors.

---

[32] For the values that are fixed ex ante, an evaluation of data source, assumptions applied, calculations, and overall appropriateness will be conducted during the validation.

Information on all monitoring points need to be included in the monitoring plan. This includes the type and specification of monitoring equipment that will be used. In addition, each monitoring point should be illustrated and described under section C.2 of the PDD. Figure 4.4 shows an example of a completed input sheet of a monitoring plan sheet using registered project ID002.[33]

Figure 4.4: Monitoring Plan Sheet (Input Sheet) of ID002

Monitoring Plan Sheet (Input Sheet) [Attachment to Project Design Document]

Table 1: Parameters to be monitored *ex post*

(a) Monitoring point No.	(b) Parameters	(c) Description of data	(d) Estimated Values	(e) Units	(f) Monitoring option	(g) Source of data	(h) Measurement methods and procedures	(i) Monitoring frequency	(j) Other comments
(1)	$EC_{PJ, i, p}$	Amount of electricity consumption of the project refrigerator *i* during the period *p*	603.0	MWh/p	Option C	Monitored data	Data is measured by measuring equipments in the factory. - Specification of measuring equipments: Electrical power meter is applied for measurement of electrical power consumption of project refrigerator. - Measuring and recording: Measured data is automatically sent to a server where data is recorded and stored. - Data collection and reporting: Inputting the collected data to a spreadsheet electronically. - QA/QC: 1) Recorded data is checked its integrity once a month by responsible staff. 2) Calibration is conducted every year after the installation by a qualified entity.	Continuously	
(2)	$EI_{grid, p}$	Electricity imported from the grid to the project site during the period *p*	603.0	MWh/p	Option B	Invoice from the power company who owns the grid	Data is collected from relevant invoices from the power company who owns the grid and input to a spreadsheet electronically.	Every month	
(3)	$h_{gen, p}$	Operating time of captive electricity generator during the period *p*	0	hours/p	Option C	Monitored data	Data is measured by meter equipped to a generator. - Specification of measuring equipments: Meter is applied for measurement of the operation time of captive electricity generator. - Measuring and recording: Measured data is recorded and stored electronically. - Data collection and reporting: Inputting the collected data to a spreadsheet electronically. - QA/QC: 1) Recorded data is checked its integrity once a month by responsible staff. 2) Calibration is conducted every year after the installation by a qualified entity.	Continuously	

continued on next page

---

[33] The Joint Crediting Mechanism. Project : ID002 Project of Introducing High Efficiency Refrigerator to a Food Industry Cold Storage in Indonesia. Accessed on 15 September 2016 at https://www.jcm.go.jp/id-jp/projects/2

Figure 4.4 *continued*

Table 2: Project-specific parameters to be fixed *ex ante*

(a) Parameters	(b) Description of data	(c) Estimated Values	(d) Units	(e) Source of data	(f) Other comments
EF_{elec}	[For grid electricity] CO_2 emission factor for consumed electricity	0.814	tCO_2/MWh	The most recent value available at the time of validation is applied and fixed for the monitoring period thereafter. The data is sourced from "Emission Factors of Electricity Interconnection Systems", National Committee on Clean Development Mechanism Indonesian DNA for CDM unless otherwise instructed by the Joint Committee.	
EF_{elec}	[For captive electricity] CO_2 emission factor for consumed electricity	0.80	tCO_2/MWh	Default value stipulated in the para.9 of CDM approved methodology AMS-I.A ver.16.	
$COP_{RE,i}$	COP of the project refrigerator type *i*	1.71	-	The default values for $COP_{RE,i}$ are set as follows: For cold storage: 1.71 For individual quick freezer: 1.32	
$COP_{PJ,i}$	COP of the reference refrigerator type *i*	2.20	-	Specifications of project refrigerator *i* prepared for the quotation or factory acceptance test data by manufacturer.	
RC_{gen}	Rated capacity of generator	200.00	kW	Specification of generator for captive electricity.	

Table3: *Ex-ante* estimation of CO_2 emission reductions

CO_2 emission reductions	Units
140	tCO_2/p

[Monitoring option]

Option A	Based on public data which is measured by entities other than the project participants (Data used: publicly recognized data such as statistical data and specifications)
Option B	Based on the amount of transaction which is measured directly using measuring equipments (Data used: commercial evidence such as invoices)
Option C	Based on the actual measurement using measuring equipments (Data used: measured values)

CDM = Clean Development Mechanism, CO_2 = carbon dioxide, COP = coefficient of performance, DNA = designated national authority, kW = kilowatt, MWh = megawatt-hour, QA/QC = quality assurance and quality control, tCO_2 = tons of carbon dioxide.

Source: The Joint Crediting Mechanism. Project : ID 002 Project of Introducing High Efficiency Refrigerator to a Food Industry Cold Storage in Indonesia. Accessed on 15 September 2016 at https://www.jcm.go.jp/id-jp/projects/2

The MPS(calc_process)provides the calculations for the reference emissions, project emissions, and net emission reductions. The calculated reference emissions, project emissions, and emission reductions will be automatically indicated in the MPS(input). Figure 4.5 shows an example of a completed MPS(calc_process).

Figure 4.5: Monitoring Plan Sheet (Calculation Process Sheet) of ID002

Monitoring Plan Sheet (Calculation Process Sheet) [Attachment to Project Design Document]

	Fuel type	Value	Units	Parameter
1. Calculations for emission reductions				
Emission reductions during the period *p*	N/A	140.7	tCO_2/p	ER_p
2. Selected default values, etc.				
COP of the reference refrigerator type *i*	N/A	1.71	-	$COP_{RE,i}$
COP of the project refrigerator type *i*	N/A	2.20	-	$COP_{PJ,i}$
3. Calculations for reference emissions				
Reference emissions during the period *p*	N/A	631.5	tCO_2/p	RE_p
CO_2 emission factor for consumed electricity [grid]	Electricity	0.814	tCO_2/MWh	EF_{elec}
CO_2 emission factor for consumed electricity [captive]	Electricity	0.80	tCO_2/MWh	EF_{elec}
Proportion of grid electricity over total electricity consumed at the project site	N/A	1.00	-	-
Proportion of captive electricity over total electricity consumed at the project site	N/A	0.00	-	-

continued on next page

Figure 4.5 *continued*

4. Calculations of the project emissions				
Project emissions during the period p		490.8	tCO$_2$/p	PE$_p$
CO$_2$ emission factor for consumed electricity [grid]	Electricity	0.814	tCO$_2$/MWh	EF$_{elec}$
CO$_2$ emission factor for consumed electricity [captive]	Electricity	0.80	tCO$_2$/MWh	EF$_{elec}$
Proportion of grid electricity over total electricity consumed at the project site	N/A	1.00	-	-
Proportion of captive electricity over total electricity consumed at the project site	N/A	0.00	-	-
Amount of electricity consumption of the project refrigerator i during the period p	Electricity	603	MWh/p	EC$_{PJ,i,p}$

[List of Default Values]

	COP$_{RE,i}$	
For cold storage	1.71	
For individual quick freezer	1.32	

CO$_2$ = carbon dioxide, COP = coefficient of performance, MWh = megawatt-hour, tCO$_2$ = tons of carbon dioxide.

Source: The Joint Crediting Mechanism. Project : ID 002 Project of Introducing High Efficiency Refrigerator to a Food Industry Cold Storage in Indonesia. Accessed on 15 September 2016 at https://www.jcm.go.jp/id-jp/projects/2

4.6.2   Monitoring Structure Sheet

The monitoring structure sheet describes the operational and management structure to be implemented in order to conduct monitoring. This is the section where the project participants establish and clearly indicate the roles and responsibilities of personnel, institutional arrangements, and procedures for data collection, archiving, and reporting of the JCM project.

The project participants should appoint a person to be responsible for monitoring activities, including the preparation of the monitoring report and managing and archiving data. The responsible person needs to ensure that the quality and content of the monitoring report meets requirements. The monitoring structure sheet also indicates the person(s) responsible for managing the monitoring points, collection of data, and maintenance and control of measuring instruments, including calibration and regular inspection. Figure 4.6 shows an example of a completed monitoring structure sheet.

Figure 4.6: Monitoring Structure Sheet of ID002

Monitoring Structure Sheet [Attachment to Project Design Document]

Responsible personnel	Role
Project Manager	Responsible for project implementation, monitoring results and reporting.
Deputy Project Manager	Appointed to be in charge of confirming the recorded data and archived data.
QA/QC team	Appointed to be in charge of checking the archived data for irregularity and calibration of the monitoring equipments.
Record keeper	Appointed to be in charge of inputting the monitored data to a spreadsheet (recording sheet) mannually

Source: The Joint Crediting Mechanism. Project : ID 002 Project of Introducing High Efficiency Refrigerator to a Food Industry Cold Storage in Indonesia. Accessed on 15 September 2016 at https://www.jcm.go.jp/id-jp/projects/2

Box 6: Important Points to Consider in Preparing the Monitoring Plan

- Approved methodology, the project design document, and monitoring guidelines should be used to develop the monitoring plan (monitoring plan sheet and monitoring structure sheet). Make sure that positioning of monitoring points as well as the types of equipment to be installed are in accordance with what's described in the monitoring plan.

- The monitoring spreadsheet should not be altered, especially the fields where automatic calculations are involved. Make sure to fill in only the appropriate input fields.

- Measuring equipment used during the monitoring must be properly calibrated in line with international standard or manufacturer's specifications as defined in the monitoring plan.

- The project participants should ensure that the monitored data required for verification and issuance is kept and archived electronically for 2 years after the final issuance of credits.

Source: Authors.

MODULE 5:
VALIDATION

5.1 INTRODUCTION TO THE MODULE

The objective of this module is to assist project participants to prepare for the validation process. This module is divided into five subsections: (5.1) Introduction to the Module, (5.2) Timeline and Process Flow, (5.3) Validation Steps, (5.4) Third-Party Entity, and (5.5) Modalities of Communication Statement.

5.2 TIMELINE AND PROCESS FLOW

Validation is the independent evaluation of a proposed Joint Crediting Mechanism (JCM) project by a third-party entity (TPE) to assess its compliance with the JCM requirements in accordance with the *Guidelines for Validation and Verification*. Validation is a requirement for every proposed JCM project, prior to registration and the project participant is responsible for engaging a TPE. The same TPE can be used for validation and verification and a project participant may undertake validation and verification simultaneously. TPEs are independent auditors designated by the respective Joint Committee to conduct validation and verification activities. Details regarding TPEs and their roles are provided in Section 5.4.

In carrying out validation work, the TPE (i) follows the *Guidelines for Validation and Verification*, other rules and guidelines, and all decisions made by the Joint Committee, and integrates its provisions into the TPE's own quality management system; (ii) assesses the accuracy, conservativeness, relevance, completeness, consistency, and transparency of the information and data provided by the project participants; and (iii) determines whether information provided by the project participant is reliable and credible.

The time required for validation depends on many factors, such as the complexity of the proposed project; the availability of the TPE, project participant, and consultant; and the number of corrective action requests (CAR), clarification requests (CL), and forward action requests (FAR) identified. Therefore, it is not possible to generalize the timeline. However, all registered projects had completed validation in less than 6 months, and a number of projects completed validation in 1–2 months.[34] Figure 5.1 summarizes the validation process.

---

[34] Calculated based on the time between the start of the public comments and the start of the completeness check.

Figure 5.1: Flowchart of the Validation Process

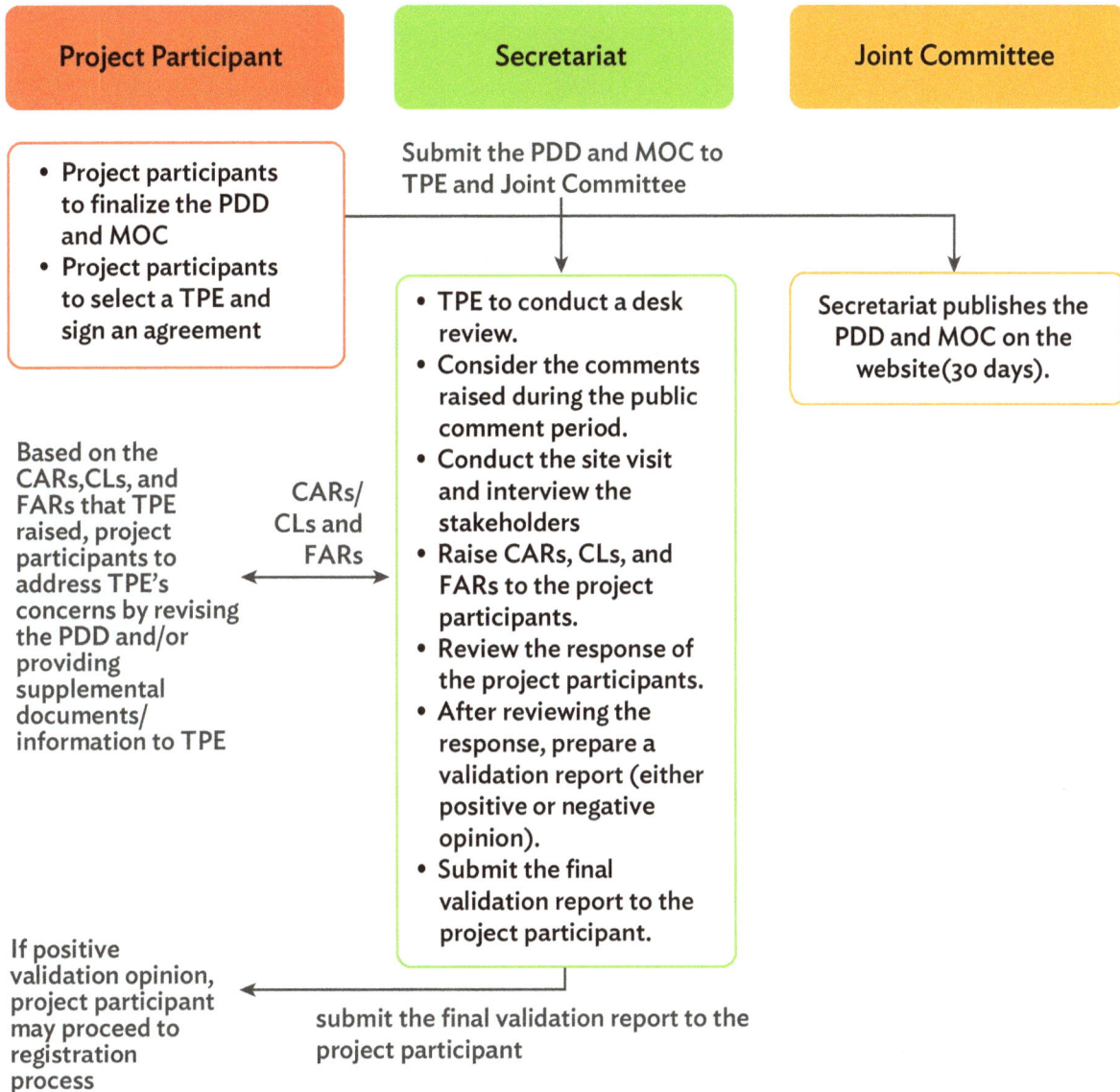

Project Participant	Secretariat	Joint Committee

Submit the PDD and MOC to TPE and Joint Committee

- Project participants to finalize the PDD and MOC
- Project participants to select a TPE and sign an agreement

- TPE to conduct a desk review.
- Consider the comments raised during the public comment period.
- Conduct the site visit and interview the stakeholders
- Raise CARs, CLs, and FARs to the project participants.
- Review the response of the project participants.
- After reviewing the response, prepare a validation report (either positive or negative opinion).
- Submit the final validation report to the project participant.

Secretariat publishes the PDD and MOC on the website(30 days).

Based on the CARs,CLs, and FARs that TPE raised, project participants to address TPE's concerns by revising the PDD and/or providing supplemental documents/ information to TPE

CARs/ CLs and FARs

If positive validation opinion, project participant may proceed to registration process

submit the final validation report to the project participant

CAR = corrective action request, CL = clarification request, FAR = forward action request, PDD = project design document, MOC = Modalities of Communication Statement, TPE = third-party entity.

Source: Authors

5.3 VALIDATION STEPS

The project participant submits the project design document (PDD), modalities of communication statement (MOC) and other supporting documents to the TPE for validation. The TPE then conducts validation (including but not limited to, desk review, site visit, interviewing stakeholders) and prepares a validation report containing the results of its assessment of the proposed project. The report is then submitted to the project participant. Unlike the Clean Development Mechanism (CDM), the TPE has no direct interaction with the Joint Committee, aside from confirming the authenticity and relevance of the public inputs received. Instead, the TPE coordinates with the project participants who in turn communicate with the Joint Committee.[35]

When the project participant submits the PDD and MOC to the TPE, a copy should also be submitted to the secretariat. The Secretariat then publishes the PDD and MOC on the JCM website of the country for a 30-day public input.[36] The proceedings of the public input period are noted by the TPE and will be considered in preparing the validation report.

During the validation process, the TPE

(i)   determines whether the proposed JCM project complies with the requirements of the applied methodology, rules, guidelines, and decisions by the Joint Committee; and

(ii)   assesses the claims and assumptions made in the PDD, MOC, and other documents submitted. The evidence used in this assessment is not limited to that provided by the project participants.

In assessing information, the TPE applies the means of validation specified under the *Guidelines for Validation and Verification* including but not limited to

(i)   document review,

(ii)   follow-up actions (e.g., on-site visit and telephone and/or e-mail interviews) whenever required, and

(iii)   referencing available information relating to projects or technologies similar to the proposed JCM project that are under validation or registered.

Document review involves the review of information and data provided in the PDD and its supporting documentation. Cross checks between information provided by the project participants and other information sources is also done, as well as independent background investigations if necessary.

A site visit will be carried out as part of the validation process. In cases where there is no site visit, the reasons for this need to be justified by the TPE in the validation report.

The TPE may apply a sampling approach as deemed appropriate. The TPE samples must be in line with the *Standard: Sampling and surveys for CDM project activities and programmes of activities.*[37]

---

[35]   In some host countries, it is coordinated through the secretariat.

[36]   In the case of Indonesia, a sustainable development implementation plan (SDIP) needs to be prepared and submitted to the secretariat together with the PDD. For details, please refer to the *Joint Creding Mechanism Project Cycle Procedure* and the *Joint Crediting Mechanism Guidelines for Developing Sustainable Development Implementation Plan and Report* for Indonesia. The SDIP needs to be reviewed by the secretariat.

[37]   Clean Development Mechanism. 2009. Standard: Sampling and surveys for CDM project activities and progremmes of activities. Accessed 15 September 2016 at http://cdm.unfccc.int/sunsetcms/storage/contents/stored-file-20151023110717966/meth_stan05. pdf

Public inputs received during the 30-day public comment period will be published on the JCM website of the host country, after the TPE reviews the authenticity of the comments. The TPE then assesses the comments and confirms that the inputs received have been taken into account by the project participant.

5.3.1 Corrective Action Requests, Clarification Requests, and Forward Action Requests

During the validation process, the TPE informs the project participants if issues that have been identified require further elaboration or correction in order to determine whether the project meets the validation requirements. The TPE may raise requests depending on the issues identified as shown in Table 5.1:

Table 5.1: Corrective Action Requests, Clarification Requests, and Forward Action Requests

Type of Request	Response Required to Resolve the Issue
1. Clarification Request (CL) The TPE raises a clarification request if the information provided by the project participants is insufficient or unclear and the TPE is unable to establish whether requirements of the applied methodology and guidelines have been met.	Project participants must modify the PDD or provide additional explanations that satisfy the JCM requirements.
2. Corrective Action Request (CAR) A CAR is raised by the TPE if • noncompliance with the methodology rules and guidelines has been identified, or if the evidence to prove conformity is insufficient; • mistakes have been made in applying assumptions, data, or calculations that will impair the estimate of emission reductions; or • there is a risk that emission reductions cannot be monitored or calculated.	Project participants must provide additional explanations or revise the PDD to satisfy the TPE's concerns.
3. Forward Action Request (FAR) A FAR is raised on issues relating to project implementation that require further review during the first and subsequent verifications of the project. If they have not been resolved, then the TPE will issue a CAR as part of the verification findings. The CAR will require a response from the project participants the same as any other issues raised during verification.	Project participants must resolve the FAR issue prior to verification to avoid being issued a CAR and delaying the verification process.

PDD = project design document, JCM = Joint Crediting Mechanism, TPE = third-party entity.
Source: Adapted from the Joint Crediting Mechanism guidelines for Validation and Verification.

The TPE ensures that these issues are accurately identified, discussed, clarified, addressed in the PDD, and concluded in the validation report. The TPE resolves or "closes out" CARs and CLs only if the project participants modify the project design, rectify the PDD, or provide additional explanations or evidence that satisfies the TPE's concerns. If this is not done, the TPE does not provide a positive validation opinion.

5.2.2 Validation Report

The TPE reports on all CARs, CLs, and FARs that are identified during the validation in its validation report. The validation report states either of the following final validation opinions:

(i)   a positive validation opinion, or

(ii)   a negative validation opinion explaining the reason for its opinion if the TPE determines that either the proposed JCM project does not fulfil the applicable JCM requirements or the information provided by the project participants is insufficient.

The following information is provided in a validation report:

(i)   a summary of the validation process and its conclusions;

(ii)   all its applied approaches, findings, and conclusions;

(iii) information on public comments carried out by the Joint Committee, including dates and how comments received have been taken into account by the project participants;

(iv) responses of the project participants to CARs and CLs, and discussions on and revisions to project documentation;

(v)   a list of interviewees and documents reviewed;

(vi) details of the validation team, technical experts, and internal technical reviewers involved, together with their roles in the validation activity and details of who conducted the on-site visit;

(vii) information on quality control within the team and in the validation process; and

(viii) appointment certificates or curricula vitae of the TPE's validation team members, technical experts, and internal technical reviewers for the project.

The validation report along with the supporting documents is provided to the project participants by the TPE.[38]

5.4 THIRD-PARTY ENTITY

The TPEs are independent auditors designated by the Joint Committee to conduct validation and verification activities under the JCM.

TPEs are accredited by the Joint Committee of the respective host country. The TPEs are accredited according to their expertise (sectoral experience), and are either entities accredited under ISO 14065 or designated operational entities accredited by the Executive Board under the CDM. There are a number of issues to be considered for the selection of TPE. Table 5.2 lists accredited TPEs in JCM host countries.

---

[38]   In the case of Bangladesh, the TPE should submit the validation report to the Joint Committee and project participants.

Table 5.2: Accredited Third-Party Entities in Host Countries

Third-Party Entity	Bangladesh	Cambodia	Indonesia	Lao PDR	Maldives	Mongolia	Myanmar	Palau	Thailand	Viet Nam	Others*
Bureau Veritas Certification Holding		x		x					x		
Deloitte Tohmatsu Evaluation and Certification Organization		x	x	x		x				x	
EPIC Sustainability Services	x	x	x	x	x	x		x		x	x
ERM Certification and Verification Services			x			x					x
Japan Management Association	x	x	x	x	x	x		x		x	x
Japan Quality Assurance Organization	x	x	x	x	x	x		x		x	x
KBS Certification Services	x	x	x	x	x	x		x		x	x
Lloyd's Register Quality Assurance	x	x	x	x	x	x		x	x	x	x
Mutuagung Lestari			x								
National Renewable Energy Center						x					
SGS United Kingdom						x					
TUV Rheinland (China)	x		x		x	x		x		x	x
TUV Rheinland Indonesia			x								
TÜV SÜD South Asia	x		x			x				x	
URS Verification						x					

DMC = developing member country, JCM = Joint Crediting Mechanism, Lao PDR = Lao People's Democratic Republic.

* Others include non-DMC JCM member partners such as Chile, Costa Rica, Ethiopia, Kenya, Mexico, and Saudi Arabia.

Source: The Joint Crediting Mechanism. Accessed on 15 September 2016 at https://www.jcm.go.jp/

Project participants should consider how they intend to work with a TPE. Communicating openly and in a timely fashion will assist the TPE in completing the validation and verification process. Project participants can also help by ensuring that the TPE has timely access to information, records, personnel, or stakeholders that the TPE requires to complete verification.

The TPE selection process is an important step and the project entity should consider multiple TPEs. Timely engagement of the TPE and close coordination with them throughout the process will help progress the project to the registration and/or JCM credit issuance stage. Box 7 provides some points that project entities should consider while making the selection.

Box 7: Items to Consider in Selecting Third-Party Entities

- Review the TPE's ability to complete the validation and verification by reviewing its specific sectoral scope (some TPEs are eligible to work only on certain sectoral scope[s]) and experience on the JCM website https://www.jcm.go.jp/

- A track record of CDM validation and verification could be an indicator of the TPE's experience.

- If possible, find out if past clients were satisfied with their experience.

- Check for fluency in the local language or country experience for better communication. Language skills are important as the TPE will need to speak to team members (including site personnel) to verify information for data collection, equipment calibration, training, etc., while some documents (e.g., national laws and regulations) are often available only in the local language.

- Request information on the team composition in terms of internal and external experts. Internal experts are preferable to external experts as they will be available and committed up to the completion of the job.

- Confirm the availability of the TPE resource persons (including for site visits) and their commitment to the timeline.

- Discuss and work out an indicative work schedule on the validation and verification timeline with the TPE before signing the contract with the TPE.

- A project participant should consider at least two TPEs before signing a contract with one of them.

CDM = Clean Development Mechanism, JCM = Joint Crediting Mechanism, TPE = third-party entity.
Source: Authors.

5.5   MODALITIES OF COMMUNICATION STATEMENT

The modalities of communication statement (MOC), a prescribed form, identifies the focal point of a JCM project designated to communicate with the secretariat and the Joint Committee on behalf of all of the project participants.[39]

For each proposed JCM project, the project participant is required to complete the MOC form and submit it together with the PDD to the secretariat. The secretariat publishes the submitted MOC on the JCM website upon registration of the project. Only sections 1 to 4 of the MOC, without the specimen signatures, are made publicly available. The complete MOC is shared only among the project participants, the Joint Committee, the secretariat, and the engaged TPE.

The focal point entity has the sole authority to communicate with the secretariat in relation to (a) requests for issuance of credits to respective accounts; (b) requests for addition and/or voluntary withdrawal of project participants and focal points, as well as changes to company names, legal status, contact details, and specimen signatures; (c) all other project-related matters not covered by (a) or (b) above, e.g., validation, registration, verification, issuance of credits, or post-registration changes to the JCM project.

---

[39]   In the case of Bangladesh, there must be two focal points and at least one must be from Bangladesh. In the case of Indonesia, multiple entities can become focal points.

During the validation process, the TPE is required to conduct a thorough assessment of the information contained within the MOC as follows:

(i)   The TPE validates the corporate and personal identities of all project participants and the focal point through

    a.   directly checking evidence for corporate, personal identity, and other relevant documentation;

    b.   notarized documentation; or

    c.   written confirmation from the project participants that all corporate and personal details, including specimen signatures, are valid and accurate.

(ii)   When the TPE validates identity, the TPE ensures that the official who submits the MOC to the TPE and the official who signed the written confirmation (if a different person) is/are duly authorized to do so on behalf of the project participants.

(iii)   The TPE ensures that the MOC is received from a project participant with whom the TPE has a contractual relationship.

(iv)   The TPE also checks that

    a.   the latest version of the form for the MOC has been used, and

    b.   the information required as per the form for the MOC is correctly completed.

The MOC form is available for download from the JCM website of each country under the Rules and Guidelines subsection of each of the country-specific sections. An example of an MOC form is included in Appendix 6.

MODULE 6:
REGISTRATION

6.1   INTRODUCTION TO THE MODULE

The objective of this module is to instruct project participants on what to do after successfully completing the validation in order to have their project registered. This module is divided into two subsections: (6.1) Introduction to the Module, and (6.2) Registration Process.

6.2   REGISTRATION PROCESS

Registration is the Joint Committee's formal acceptance of a validated project as a Joint Crediting Mechanism (JCM) project activity. It is a prerequisite for the certification and issuance of JCM credits relating to that project activity.[40] Therefore, registration is a key stage in the JCM project cycle, as it is when the project becomes eligible to generate JCM credits. Figure 6.1 outlines the registration process.

---

[40]   In the JCM, validation and verification may be undertaken simultaneously. Hence unlike in the CDM, registration is not a prerequisite for verification.

Figure 6.1: Flowchart of the Registration Process

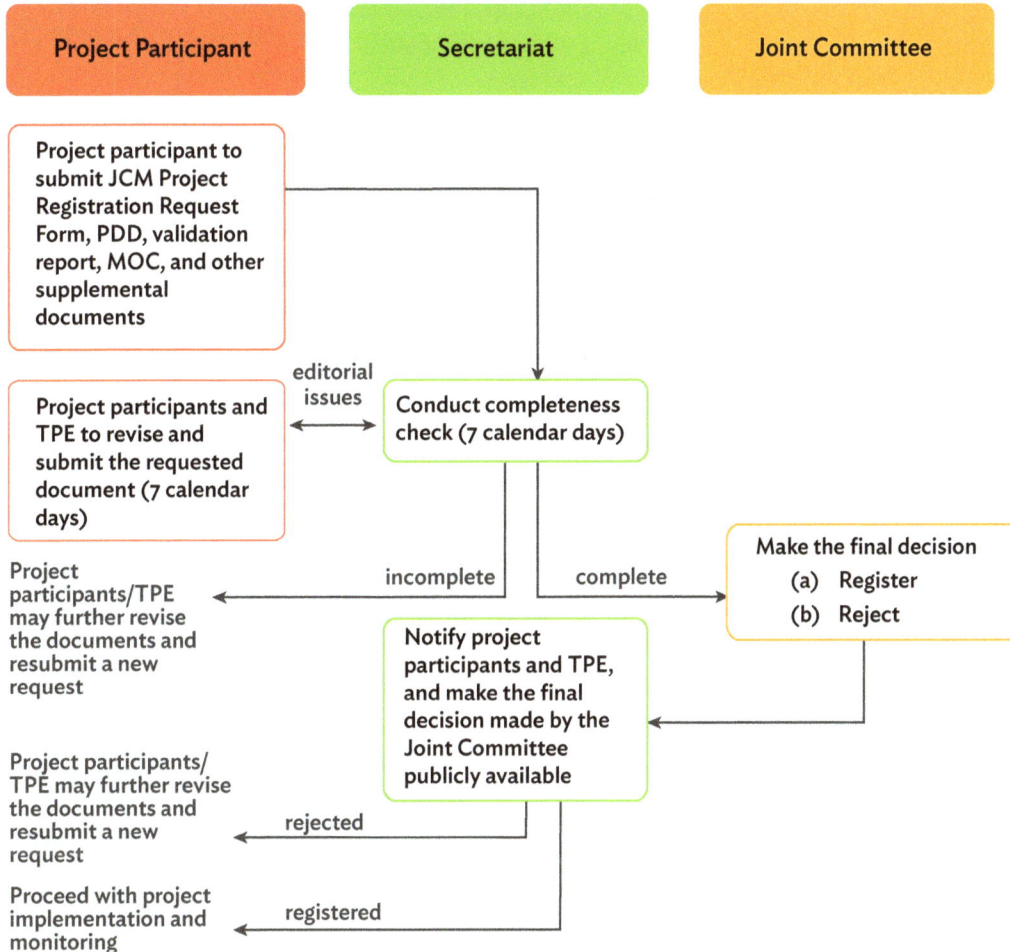

Project Participant	Secretariat	Joint Committee

Project participant to submit JCM Project Registration Request Form, PDD, validation report, MOC, and other supplemental documents

editorial issues

Project participants and TPE to revise and submit the requested document (7 calendar days)

Conduct completeness check (7 calendar days)

Project participants/TPE may further revise the documents and resubmit a new request

incomplete

complete

Make the final decision
(a) Register
(b) Reject

Notify project participants and TPE, and make the final decision made by the Joint Committee publicly available

Project participants/ TPE may further revise the documents and resubmit a new request

rejected

Proceed with project implementation and monitoring

registered

JCM = Joint Crediting Mechanism, MOC = modalities of communication statement, PDD = project design document, TPE = third-party entity.

Source: Authors.

6.2.1 Submission of the Request for Registration

To request registration, the focal point entity submits the completed JCM Project Registration Request Form,[41] the validated project design document (PDD), modalities of communication statement (MOC), validation report (with positive validation opinion), and other supporting documents, as appropriate, to the Joint Committee[42] through the secretariat by electronic means.

---

[41] A sample JCM Project Registration Request Form is provided in Appendix 7.
[42] In the case of Indonesia, a positively reviewed SDIP should be submitted as part of the request for registration.

6.2.2 Completeness Check

Upon receiving the request for registration, the secretariat conducts a completeness check within 7 calendar days to determine whether the documents submitted in relation to the request are complete.

If the secretariat finds issues that are editorial in nature, the secretariat requests the project participants to submit the missing or revised documents and/or information. This must occur within 7 calendar days after receipt of the request for registration. The project participants must then submit the requested documents and/or information within 7 calendar days. If the response is not made within the given time, the secretariat deems the request for registration to be incomplete.

If the secretariat concludes that the request for registration does not meet the requirements of the completeness check, the secretariat communicates the underlying reasons to the project participants, and the TPE publishes the same on the JCM website.

If the request for registration is incomplete, the project participants may resubmit the request for registration together with the completed requirements and corrected documents as appropriate.

6.2.3 Conclusion on the Request for Registration

Upon positive conclusion of the completeness check, the Joint Committee decides whether to register the proposed JCM project.[43]

If the Joint Committee decides to register the proposed JCM project, the secretariat notifies the host country government, the Government of Japan, the project participants, and the TPE of the registration and makes the relevant information on the project publicly available through the JCM website.

If the Joint Committee rejects the request for registration, the secretariat notifies the project participants and the TPE of the rejection and its reasons, and makes the decision with its reasons publicly available through the JCM website.

The project participants may resubmit the request for registration with revised documentation if the reasons for the rejection can be addressed by means of a revised validation report based on a revised PDD.

---

[43]   In the case of Indonesia, there will be an additional review process by the secretariat after the completeness check. For details, please refer to the *Joint Crediting Mechanism Project Cycle Procedure* for Indonesia.

MODULE 7:
MONITORING AND REPORTING

7.1 INTRODUCTION TO THE MODULE

The objective of this module is to explain Joint Crediting Mechanism (JCM) monitoring requirements. Monitoring is the responsibility of the project participants, and JCM credits cannot be verified and issued to a project unless proper monitoring is conducted. The module also introduces common issues and concerns that may arise in the monitoring process. This module is divided into three subsections: (7.1) Introduction to the Module, (7.2) Monitoring Report, (7.3) Monitoring, and (7.4) Monitoring Issues.

7.2 MONITORING REPORT

Once the project is operational, the project participant is responsible for monitoring and recording the data. At the end of the monitoring period this information is input into a monitoring report using the monitoring report sheet of the registered project design document (PDD).[44]

The monitoring period is the period of time over which monitoring takes place for each monitoring report. There are no requirements on how long a monitoring period must be, and it is up to the project participants to decide based on their own assessment. However, in many cases, the cost of verification and expected emission reduction influences the monitoring period. For example, small projects tend to set a longer monitoring period to reduce the total verification cost.

7.2.1 Monitoring Report Sheet (input sheet)

The monitoring report sheet consists of an input sheet (MRS [input]) and a calculation process sheet (MRS [calc_process]). The project participant enters all information into the MRS(input) spreadsheet and the emission reduction calculations will be done in the MRS (calc_procrss) worksheet. For each parameter in the MRS(input), the project participants should provide the following information:

- Monitoring period: Describe the monitoring period,
- Monitored values: Provide the values of the monitored parameter for the purpose of calculating emission reductions,
- Monitoring option: Fill in the monitoring option used (option A, B, and C as described in Section 4.6.1),

---

- Source of data: Provide the source of data used. Clearly indicate the type of data source (e.g., logbooks, daily records, surveys, etc.) and the spatial level of data (e.g., local, regional, national, international), if applicable,

- Measurement methods and procedures: Describe how the parameters are measured or calculated (e.g., using SCADA system) including quality assurance and quality control (QA/QC) procedures applied (e.g., installation of a backup meter and cross checking with the main meter). If the parameter is measured, describe the equipment used to measure it, including details on accuracy level and calibration information (frequency, date of calibration, and validity),

- Monitoring frequency: Describe the monitoring frequency,

- Other comments: Additional information, if applicable.

Figure 7.1 contains an example from a JCM project that has successfully had credits issued, ID002 *Project of Introducing High Efficiency Refrigerator to a Food Industry Cold Storage in Indonesia.*[45] Table 1 of the MRS(input) is filled out based on the data and information monitored.

45   The Joint Crediting Mechanism. Project : ID002 Project of Introducing High Efficiency Refrigerator to a Food Industry Cold Storage in Indonesia. Accessed on September 15 2016 at https://www.jcm.go.jp/id-jp/projects/2

Figure 7.1: *Monitoring Report Sheet (Input Sheet) of Project ID002: Project of Introducing High Efficiency Refrigerator to a Food Industry Cold Storage in Indonesia*

Monitoring Report Sheet (Input Sheet) [For Verification]

Table 1: Parameters monitored ex post

(a) Monitoring period	(b) Monitoring point No.	(c) Parameters	(d) Description of data	(e) Estimated Values	(f) Units	(g) Monitoring option	(h) Source of data	(i) Measurement methods and procedures	(j) Monitoring frequency	(k) Other comments
From 2015/2/2 until 2015/7/31	(1)	$EC_{PJ,i,p}$	Amount of electricity consumption of the project refrigerator *i* during the period *p*	126.351	MWh/p	Option C	Monitored data	Data is measured by measuring equipments in the factory. - Specification of measuring equipments: Electrical power meter is applied for measurement of electrical power consumption of project refrigerator. - Measuring and recording: Measured data is automatically sent to a server where data is recorded and stored. - Data collection and reporting: Inputting the recorded data to a spreadsheet electrically. - QA/QC: 1) Recorded data is checked its integrity once a month by responsible	Continuously	
From 2015/2/1 until 2015/7/31	(2)	$EI_{grid,p}$	Electricity imported from the grid to the project site during the period *p*	647.192	MWh/p	Option B	Invoice from the power company	Data is collected and recorded from invoices from the power company.	Every month	
From 2015/2/1 until 2015/7/31	(3)	$h_{gen,p}$	Operating time of captive electricity generator during the period *p*	24.0	hours/p	Option C	Monitored data	Data is measured by meter equipped to a generator. - Specification of measuring equipments: Meter is applied for measurement of the operation time of captive electricity generator. - Measuring and recording: Measured data is recorded and stored electrically. - Data collection and reporting: Inputting the recorded data to a spreadsheet electrically. - QA/QC: 1) Recorded data is checked its integrity once a month by responsible	Continuously	

continued on next page

Figure 7.1 continued

Table 2: Project-specific parameters fixed ex ante

(a) Parameters	(b) Description of data	(c) Estimated Values	(d) Units	(e) Source of data	(f) Other comments
EF_{elec}	[For grid electricity] CO_2 emission factor for consumed electricity	0.814	tCO_2/MWh	The most recent value available at the time of validation is applied and fixed for the monitoring period thereafter. The data is sourced from "Emission Factors of Electricity Interconnection Systems", National Committee on Clean Development Mechanism Indonesian DNA for CDM unless otherwise instructed by the Joint Committee.	
EF_{elec}	[For captive electricity] CO_2 emission factor for consumed electricity	0.800	tCO_2/MWh	Default value stipulated in the para.9 of CDM approved methodology AMS-I.A ver.16.	
$COP_{RE,i}$	COP of the project refrigerator type i	1.710	-	The default values for COPRE,i are set as follows: For cold storage: 1.71 For individual quick freezer: 1.32	
$COP_{PJ,i}$	COP of the reference refrigerator type i	2.200	-	Specifications of project refrigerator i prepared for the quotation or factory acceptance test data by manufacturer.	
RC_{gen}	Rated capacity of generator	220.000	kW	Specification of generator for captive electricity.	

Table3: Ex-post calculation of CO_2 emission reductions

Monitoring Period	CO_2 emission reductions	Units
From 2015/2/2 until 2015/7/31	29	tCO_2/p

[Monitoring option]

Option A	Based on public data which is measured by entities other than the project participants (Data used: publicly recognized data such as statistical data and
Option B	Based on the amount of transaction which is measured directly using measuring equipments (Data used: commercial evidence such as invoices)
Option C	Based on the actual measurement using measuring equipments (Data used: measured values)

kW = kilowatt, MWh = megawatt-hour, tCO_2 = tons of carbon dioxide.

Source: The Joint Crediting Mechanism. Project : ID 002 Project of Introducing High Efficiency Refrigerator to a Food Industry Cold Storage in Indonesia. Accessed on 15 September 2016 at https://www.jcm.go.jp/id-jp/projects/2

7.2.2   Monitoring Report Sheet (calculation process sheet)

The MRS(calc_process) calculates the reference emissions, project emissions, and emission reductions for a specific time period based on the data input in the MRS(input). The calculations are built into this spreadsheet and project participants are not required to take any action on this sheet. Figure 7.2 is an example of MRS(calc_process) from the same project, ID002 *Project of Introducing High Efficiency Refrigerator to a Food Industry Cold Storage in Indonesia*. Red boxes in the figure indicate calculated emission reductions, reference emissions, and project emissions.

Figure 7.2: Monitoring Report Sheet (Calculation Process Sheet) of Project ID002

Monitoring Report Sheet (Calculation Process Sheet) [For Verification]

	Fuel type	Value	Units	Parameter
1. Calculations for emission reductions				
Emission reductions during the period p	N/A	29.5	tCO_2/p	ER_p
2. Selected default values, etc.				
COP of the reference refrigerator type i	N/A	1.71	-	$COP_{RE,i}$
COP of the project refrigerator type i	N/A	2.20	-	$COP_{PJ,i}$
3. Calculations for reference emissions				
Reference emissions during the period p	N/A	132.3	tCO_2/p	RE_p
CO_2 emission factor for consumed electricity [grid]	Electricity	0.814	tCO_2/MWh	EF_{elec}
CO_2 emission factor for consumed electricity [captive]	Electricity	0.80	tCO_2/MWh	EF_{elec}
Proportion of grid electricity over total electricity consumed at the project site	N/A	0.99	-	-
Proportion of captive electricity over total electricity consumed at the project site	N/A	0.01	-	-
Amount of electricity consumption of the project refrigerator i during the period p	Electricity	126	MWh/p	$EC_{PJ,i,p}$
COP of the reference refrigerator type i	N/A	1.71	-	$COP_{RE,i}$
COP of the project refrigerator type i	N/A	2.20	-	$COP_{PJ,i}$
4. Calculations of the project emissions				
Project emissions during the period p		102.8	tCO_2/p	PE_p
CO_2 emission factor for consumed electricity [grid]	Electricity	0.814	tCO_2/MWh	EF_{elec}
CO_2 emission factor for consumed electricity [captive]	Electricity	0.80	tCO_2/MWh	EF_{elec}
Proportion of grid electricity over total electricity consumed at the project site	N/A	0.99	-	-
Proportion of captive electricity over total electricity consumed at the project site	N/A	0.01	-	-
Amount of electricity consumption of the project refrigerator i during the period p	Electricity	126	MWh/p	$EC_{PJ,i,p}$

[List of Default Values]

	$COP_{RE,i}$	
For cold storage	1.71	
For individual quick freezer	1.32	

CO_2 = carbon dioxide, COP = coefficient of performance, MWh = megawatt-hour, tCO_2 = tons of carbon dioxide.

Source: The Joint Crediting Mechanism. Project : ID 002 Project of Introducing High Efficiency Refrigerator to a Food Industry Cold Storage in Indonesia. Accessed on 15 September 2016 at https://www.jcm.go.jp/id-jp/projects/2

7.3 MONITORING

The framework for the monitoring process is established during the PDD development stage (Module 4). It is important that project participants follow the monitoring processes laid out in the monitoring plan sheet of the registered PDD.

7.3.1 Preparing for Actual Measurement

The following information should be included under the measurement methods and procedures of the MRS(input) for each monitoring parameter:

- measurement equipment to be used,
- accuracy level,
- calibration information (frequency, date of calibration, and validity),
- measurement procedure, and
- quality assurance and quality control (QA/QC) process.

Accuracy level refers to the accuracy specification of the measuring equipment used for the monitoring. Prior to the start of operation, the project participants should confirm that the equipment meets the requirements specified in the methodology and registered PDD. If the project participants cannot find equipment with the required accuracy, higher accuracy equipment should be used.

The project participants are required to record and archive data for each of the data sources indicated in the monitoring plan of the registered PDD. These records will be used as evidence during verification, to confirm the figures used in the monitoring report.

Box 8: Recommendations for Proper Measurement and Quality Assurance and Quality Control Procedures

Proper measurement procedures and quality assurance and quality control (QA/QC) procedures are essential for good monitoring.

- Project participants should establish a JCM monitoring team and assign a responsible person for each monitoring task.
- The team should include a supervisor and a quality control person (and if applicable, an external consultant) to manage QA/QC.
- To ensure accurate record keeping, a data input system should be designed (in many cases, using Excel worksheets), which is different from the monitoring plan sheet of the Joint Crediting Mechanism, for regular recording of the measured values.
- Furthermore, the project participants should consider preparing a monitoring manual, together with a monitoring and calibration schedule, to assist the team to manage the monitoring process.

Source: Authors.

Figure 7.3: Example of a Monitoring Procedure

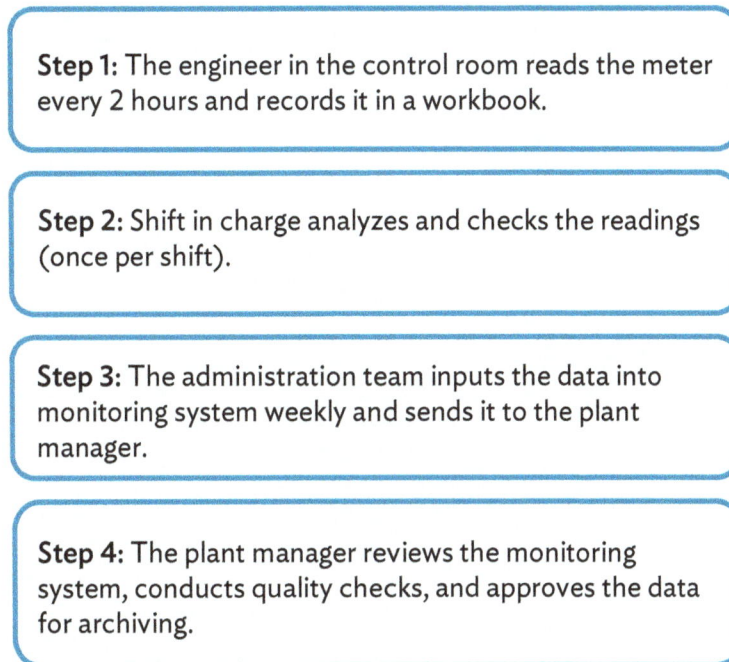

Step 1: The engineer in the control room reads the meter every 2 hours and records it in a workbook.

Step 2: Shift in charge analyzes and checks the readings (once per shift).

Step 3: The administration team inputs the data into monitoring system weekly and sends it to the plant manager.

Step 4: The plant manager reviews the monitoring system, conducts quality checks, and approves the data for archiving.

Source: Authors.

In the event that monitoring of required parameters cannot be done in accordance with the methodology or the registered PDD, the project participants must go through the post-registration project change process as explained in Module 9.

7.3.2 Calibration and Data Correction

For all measured parameters project participants are required to describe the calibration frequency of the measuring equipment in the monitoring plan in the registered PDD.

Calibration is a process that identifies the extent to which the value being recorded by a device deviates from the true value. Calibration ensures the accuracy of the measurement of the particular parameter.

Over time, an instrument's performance may gradually deviate from the stated specification. This can happen for a variety of reasons, such as mechanical wear and tear; effects of dust, fumes, and chemicals; and other factors in the operating environment. Calibration overcomes this deviation and corrects the instrument so that it gives accurate readings.

Calibration can be done in situ (with the instrument remaining in place) or the instrument can be removed and sent for full calibration at a laboratory or testing facility. Note that it is not always possible to access the meter for maintenance or calibration when the project is operational. In such cases it will be important to prioritize meter maintenance or calibration as part of planned preventative maintenance schedules and activities, or planned shutdowns.

Calibration should only be conducted by a qualified technician in consultation with the manufacturer of the instrument.

Based on the outcome of the calibration, the project participant should determine the necessity for data correction in the calculation of emission reductions as illustrated in Figure 7.4, and further explained in Box 8.

Figure 7.4: Decision Tree for Data Correction

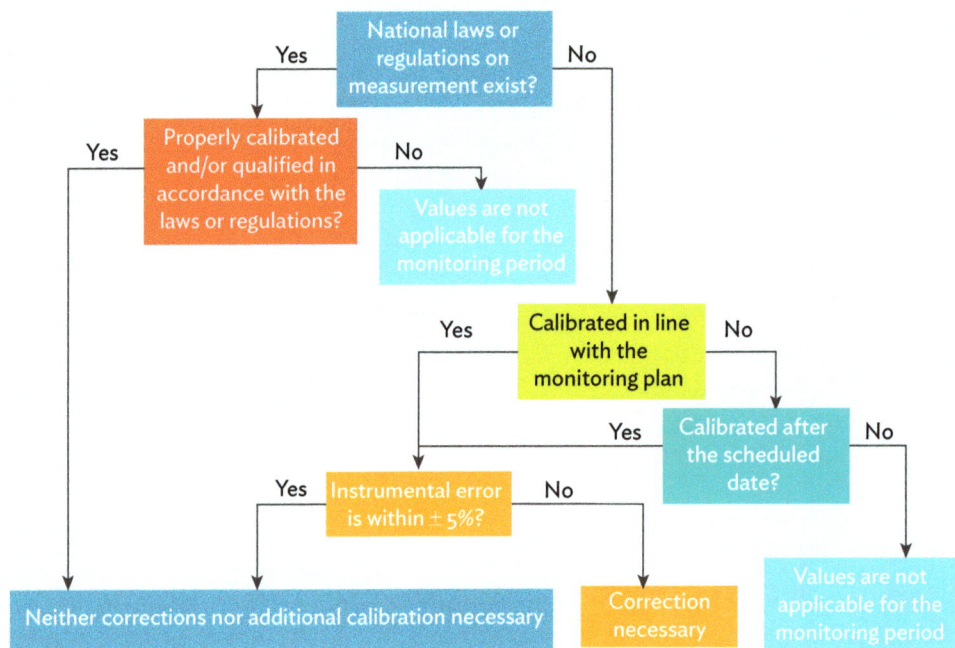

Source: *Guidelines for Developing Project Design Document and Monitoring Report.*

Box 9: Examples of How Instrumental Errors Are Addressed

A hypothetical biomass power generation project is envisaged. The project generates electricity from biomass fuel and supplies it to the grid system. The project consumes diesel oil for a start-up and an auxiliary fuel source to meet the required level of output. In this example, emission reductions are calculated as the difference between reference emissions (calculated by multiplying electricity generated and emission factor of the grid) and project emissions (calculated by multiplying diesel oil consumed and its emission factor).

If the instrumental errors identified in the calibration test do not exceed ±5%, then no correction is needed (Example 1).

Example 1: When the instrumental errors identified in the calibration test do not exceed ±5%

Measured	Parameter	Error identified during (delayed) calibration	Applied values
100 MWh	Electricity supplied to the grid (required parameter for calculating reference emissions)	±0.2%	100 MWh (uncorrected); since the error identified by calibration is less than or equal to the required accuracy level of ±5%, no correction is needed.
800 liters of diesel	Diesel flow to the power plant (required parameter for calculating project emissions)	±2%	800 liters (uncorrected); since the error identified by calibration is less than or equal to the required accuracy level of ±5%, no correction is needed.

If the instrumental errors identified in the calibration test exceeds ±5%, then a correction to the measured values is applied. The degree of correction is the identified errors minus 5%, in a way that results in a conservative calculation of emission reductions (Example 2).

Example 2: When the instrumental errors identified in the calibration test exceed ±5%

Measured	Parameter	Error identified during (delayed) calibration	Applied values
100 MWh	Electricity supplied to the grid (required parameter for calculating reference emissions)	±7%	100 MWh x (1−(7%−5%)) = 98 MWh, since the error identified by calibration is more than the required accuracy level of ±5%, and it is conservative to take the lower end of the corrected value.
800 liters of diesel	Diesel flow to the power plant (required parameter for calculating project emissions)	±10%	800 liters x (1+(10%−5%)) = 840 liters, since the error identified by calibration is more than the required accuracy level of ±5%, and it is conservative to take the higher end of the corrected value.

MWh = megawatt-hour.
Source: *The Joint Crediting Mechanism Guidelines for Developing Project Design Document and Monitoring Report.*

If monitoring equipment is not calibrated in accordance with the national laws and regulations or the monitoring plan, or if the equipment is not calibrated at all, the project participants cannot use the measured values as part of their monitoring plan, and therefore could potentially not claim emission reductions for the monitoring period.

7.4   MONITORING ISSUES

This section discusses common issues and concerns that may arise in the monitoring process. Understanding common issues will assist the project participants to mitigate and resolve issues. The issues discussed have been drawn from the monitoring or verification process under the CDM as there are few examples of monitoring and verification processes under the JCM.

7.4.1   Issue 1: Poorly Installed and Tagged Monitoring Equipment

Monitoring equipment should be properly installed and tagged. This will allow maintenance personnel to easily identify the equipment they must quality control check. Quality control checks are carried out according to the monitoring plan of the registered PDD. The location of the equipment—i.e., the point at which the parameter is being monitored—must also be consistent with the monitoring plan.

Access to the equipment should also be considered especially for ongoing verification. The TPE may want to physically verify the location of a meter and check the local display.

7.4.2   Issue 2: Selection of Monitoring Equipment

The selection of appropriate monitoring equipment and monitoring system plays an important part in the successful monitoring of a project.

When selecting equipment, the project participants have to consider many factors including the accuracy of the data that will be provided by the equipment, cost of the equipment, whether a backup meter is required, and human resources available to undertake monitoring, as well as other practical issues.

Some specific issues to consider when selecting equipment include the following:

Frequency of monitoring

It must be determined whether the monitoring is to be done on a continuous, intermittent, daily, weekly, monthly, or annual basis. This will help to determine whether it is most cost-effective to hire, lease, or buy the equipment. In certain cases, it may be possible and more cost-effective to engage an accredited or approved laboratory to carry out periodic measurements if this is all that is required. The required monitoring frequency should have been defined in the methodology or the monitoring plan. It should follow the requirements of relevant national standards of the host country. In the absence of a national standard, the international standard can be followed.

Use of the data and risk associated with it

Many of the parameters that are required to be measured as part of the monitoring plan are also required to be measured for other purposes. This will influence the type of equipment selected, particularly if the parameter being measured relates to project revenue. For example, for a renewable energy project, one of the key JCM monitoring parameters is the net electricity generation. The same parameters will also be the key monitoring requirement under the power purchase agreement that determines the project's revenue. Equipment will need to be of high accuracy and quality to minimize the risk of inaccurate or incorrect measurements and the project participant will usually have strict monitoring requirements under the power purchase agreement to comply with. It is likely that the equipment would have been selected for compliance with the power purchase agreement, and will be used for the JCM as a secondary purpose. This is acceptable, provided that this was considered in the monitoring plan.

Accuracy of the measurement

The required accuracy of measurement is predefined in national laws or regulations or in the monitoring plan. It is critical that project participants select monitoring equipment that meets the requirements of these. The required accuracy of the measurement is usually a key determinant of the cost of the equipment. The accuracy of the equipment will determine the degree of accuracy to which emission reductions can be measured.

Equipment technical specifications

This includes the range and whether the equipment is analog or digital. In some cases, this will be defined in the monitoring plan. The project participants must select equipment appropriate for the parameter being measured and the specific requirements of the project, and at an appropriate cost.

Backup meter

For critical parameters it is recommended that a backup meter be installed in order to continue monitoring in the event that the main meter fails. Typically, the need for a backup meter would have been defined in the monitoring plan as part of QA/QC procedures.

Availability of a calibration and maintenance facility within the country

Project participants need to consider whether there is an appropriate calibration and maintenance facility, including qualified personnel, within the country where the project is situated. The facility and personnel need to be qualified to calibrate the particular type or brand of equipment. If facilities and personnel are not available, then equipment will need to be sent overseas—this can be a costly and time-consuming option. If the equipment price is low, the project participants may also consider purchasing new equipment each year if the purchase is cheaper than calibration costs.

Specialized training

Some monitoring instruments are sophisticated and require specialized training in order to operate them effectively. Project participants should consider the capacity of local staff to undertake training and to subsequently operate monitoring instruments. If local capacity is insufficient, then the project may need to recruit international experts to assist.

Applicable standards

Selection of instrument standards is an important aspect of monitoring. Where possible, national standards should be selected as the testing and compliance personnel and infrastructure will be more readily available. However, in the absence of such national standards, relevant international standards may be followed for selecting an instrument.

Use of old equipment

Many project owners prefer to use old monitoring equipment available to them from previous projects, other sections of the plant, or equipment that was previously used as backup. Project participants typically do this due to cost considerations, particularly if the monitoring equipment is only used for JCM purposes and not for the plant's day-to-day operations.

If project participants do use old equipment, then it is important to first check the availability of documentation such as calibration records and specifications. If supporting documentation is not available, then using old monitoring equipment is not advised.

7.4.3 Issue 3: Ensuring the Quality of the Data Collected

To ensure the quality of the data collected is to a sufficient level of accuracy, it is useful to consider the *Guidelines for Validation and Verification* for the TPEs. Understanding the guidelines and standards applicable to TPEs in the verification process is critical to saving time and resources from incorrect or inaccurate monitoring.

A TPE undertaking data checks and calculations will use the instructions listed below. Please note these instructions aim to assist project participants better understand the TPE's role—these steps do not need to be undertaken by the project participants themselves.

- Determine whether a complete set of data is available that covers the whole monitoring period. If only partial data is available because some parameters have not been monitored in accordance with the registered monitoring plan, the TPE then opts to either give a negative verification opinion for that time period during which the data are unavailable or seek guidance from the Joint Committee.
- Cross-check the information provided in the monitoring report against other sources such as original data collection sheets, logbooks, inventories, purchase records, laboratory analysis, etc.
- Confirm that the calculations have been carried out in accordance with the formulas and methods described in the monitoring plan and the applied methodology.
- Confirm whether assumptions (if any) used in emission calculations have been justified.
- Confirm whether emission factors, default values, and other reference values (if applicable) have been correctly applied.

Project participants in some cases record monitoring data in hard copy (e.g., logbooks) and subsequently transcribe the data to an electronic format such as databases or data sheets. If project participants do transcribe data, care must be taken to ensure that the transcription process is accurate.

To manage this risk, the monitoring plan should include a QA/QC procedure that checks the accuracy of the data transfer process. Internal audits can also be useful to identify errors ahead of external verification. Even if these measures are not specified in the monitoring plan, it is recommended that they be put into place when the monitoring plan is implemented. The more accurate the data that is collected, the fewer issues that are likely to arise during verification.

MODULE 8:
VERIFICATION AND ISSUANCE

8.1 INTRODUCTION TO THE MODULE

The objective of this module is to provide project participants with information necessary to be prepared for the verification process. This module is divided into six subsections: (8.1) Introduction to the Module; (8.2) Verification; (8.3) Timing of Verification; (8.4) Corrective Action Requests, Clarification Requests, and Forward Action Requests; (8.5) Verification Report; and (8.6) Issuance of Credits. Selection of third-party entity (TPE) for verification is covered in Section 5.4 of the handbook.

8.2 VERIFICATION

Verification is the ex post independent review by a TPE of the monitoring report and the monitored greenhouse gas (GHG) emission reductions claimed by a registered Joint Crediting Mechanism (JCM) project for a specific monitoring period. Verification includes the assessment of the monitoring report to verify that it is in accordance with the corresponding methodology, along with the registered project design document (PDD),[46] validation report, all previous verification reports, applied methodology, any other information and references relevant to the project's emission reductions,[47] and the written confirmation of the avoidance of double registration.

Verification includes assessment of the following main criteria:

- the eligibility criteria stipulated in the applied methodology of implemented projects are satisfied,
- the data used in monitoring reports is credible and reliable,
- double counting of emissions is avoided, and
- there are no post-registration changes that prevent the use of the applied methodology or impact the project in other ways.[48]

The TPE prepares a report to reflect the results of the verification and sends the report to the project participants. The verification report will be the basis for the request for issuance of credits. Figure 8.1 shows the flow of the verification process.

---

[46] If validation and verification are conducted simultaneously, it would be the validated PDD and the corresponding validation opinion.

[47] In the case of Indonesia, project participants need to submit the monitoring report and sustainable development implementation report to the Joint Committee at the start of verification for further processing. For details, please refer to the *Joint Crediting Mechanism Project Cycle Procedure* for Indonesia.

[48] In the event that post-registration change is required, TPE and project participant will be required to take appropriate steps to address these changes as discussed in Module 9.

Figure 8.1: Flowchart of the Verification Process

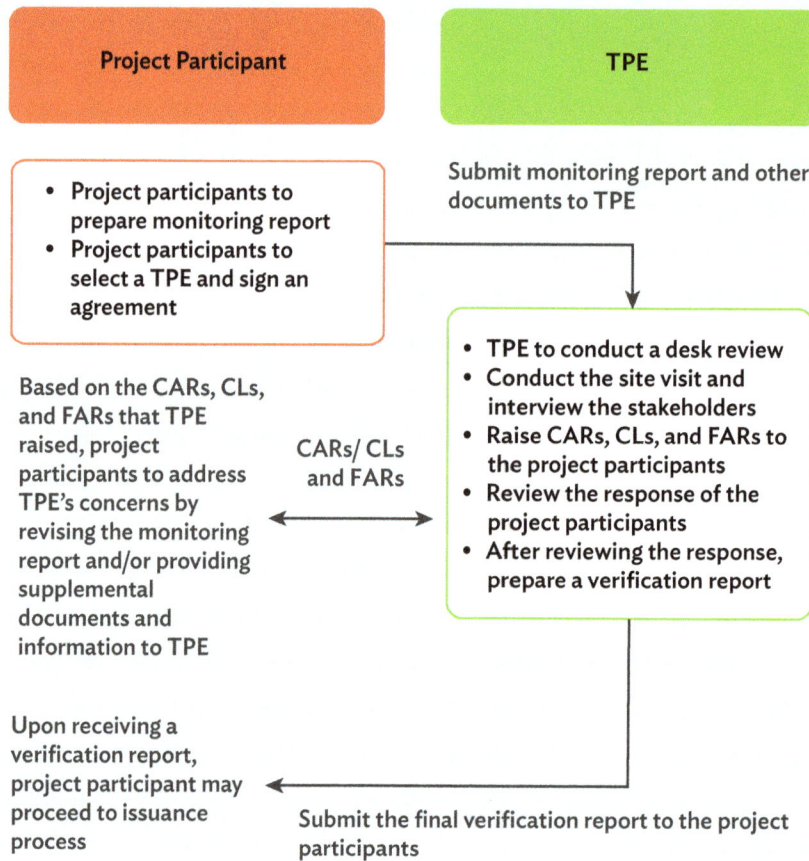

Project Participant	TPE

Submit monitoring report and other documents to TPE

- Project participants to prepare monitoring report
- Project participants to select a TPE and sign an agreement

Based on the CARs, CLs, and FARs that TPE raised, project participants to address TPE's concerns by revising the monitoring report and/or providing supplemental documents and information to TPE

CARs/ CLs and FARs

- TPE to conduct a desk review
- Conduct the site visit and interview the stakeholders
- Raise CARs, CLs, and FARs to the project participants
- Review the response of the project participants
- After reviewing the response, prepare a verification report

Upon receiving a verification report, project participant may proceed to issuance process

Submit the final verification report to the project participants

CAR = corrective action request, CL = clarification request, FAR = forward action request, TPE = third-party entity.

Source: Authors

8.3   TIMING OF VERIFICATION

There are no specific rules on when the verification has to take place, and project participants can choose the time period of the first monitoring period. Subsequent verifications and certifications can also be carried out at intervals convenient to the project participants.

Project participants may, however, consider conducting the first verification shortly after the start of operation of the JCM project. This will ensure that the project is implemented and operated according to the procedures set out in the PDD, and that any potential problems with project monitoring are addressed at an early stage.

One of the key features of the JCM is that verification can be conducted simultaneously with validation, as explained in box 1 of Module 2.

8.4   CORRECTIVE ACTION REQUESTS, CLARIFICATION REQUESTS, AND FORWARD ACTION REQUESTS

During the verification process, the TPE may make a request to the project participants that requires a response before the verification process can be finalized. This is typically done in the draft verification report, and the project participants will have the opportunity to respond to these findings and to provide further information as required. In practice, there are often several rounds of information exchange between the project participants and the TPE to reach a point where the TPE is satisfied that the issue has been resolved.

Table 8.1 contains an explanation of the types of requests a TPE can make during the verification process, including corrective action requests (CAR), clarification requests (CL), and forward action requests (FAR).

Table 8.1: Explanation of Third-Party Entity Requests in the Verification Process

Types of Request	Response Required to Resolve the Issue
1. Corrective Action Request (CAR) A CAR is raised by the TPE if: • Noncompliance with the eligibility criteria of the applied methodology are found in implementation and operation of the project, or if the evidence provided to prove conformity is insufficient. • Modifications that prevent the use of the applied methodology to the implementation, operation, and monitoring of the registered or validated project has not been sufficiently documented by the project participants.; • Mistakes have been made in applying assumptions, data, or calculations of emission reductions that will impact the quantity of emission reductions. • Issues identified in a FAR during validation or previous verification(s) to be verified have not been resolved by the project participants.	Project participants must address the issues raised to satisfy the TPE's concerns.

continued on next page

Table 8.1 *continued*

2. Clarification Request (CL) The TPE raises a CL if the information provided by the project participants is insufficient or unclear and the TPE is unable to establish whether requirements of the applied methodology, guidelines, and the PDD have been met.	Project participants must provide additional explanations to satisfy the TPE's concerns.
3. Forward Action Request (FAR) TPEs can raise FARs during verification for actions if the monitoring and reporting require attention and/or adjustment for the next verification period.	Project participants must resolve the FAR request issue for the next verification period.

TPE = third-party entity.

Source: Adapted from the Joint Crediting Mechanism Guidelines for Validation and Verification.

The TPE reports on all CARs, CLs, and FARs in its verification report, and all CARs and CLs raised during verification have to be resolved before a request for issuance of credits may be submitted.

8.5 VERIFICATION REPORT

After the verification process, the TPE will produce a verification report giving the verification conclusion and the amount of emission reductions achieved through the project if the overall verification opinion is positive. The verification report is submitted to the project participants.

The verification report has the following sections:

- A.   Summary of verification
- B.   Verification team and other experts
- C.   Means of verification, findings, and conclusions based on reporting requirements
- D.   Assessment of response to remaining issues
- E.   Verified amount of emission reductions achieved
- F.   List of interviewees and documents received

Annex. Certificates or curricula vitae of the TPE's verification team members, technical experts, and internal technical reviewers

The TPE describes in the verification report all documentation supporting verification and makes such documentation available to the Joint Committee upon request.

8.6 ISSUANCE OF CREDITS

8.6.1   Request for Issuance

Before requesting issuance of credits, project participants must have a JCM credit account opened in the registry of Japan and/or the host country where they can receive the credits. Unlike the Clean Development Mechanism (CDM), there is no central entity that issues the JCM credits. The governments of each country (Japan and the host country) issue the credits, based on notifications from the Joint Committee. The JCM credits are issued to accounts within registries that each government manages and maintains. Currently, Japan and Indonesia have established JCM registries. The process for opening an account will depend on the registry system established by each host country.[49] Project participants should therefore contact their respective secretariat or registry for guidance on opening an account.

After receiving a positive verification report and opening a JCM credit account, the project participants may request the Joint Committee through the secretariat for issuance of JCM credits. To do this, project participants must submit a completed JCM Credits Issuance Request Form, and submit it with the verified monitoring report, the verification report, and information on the allocation of credits among the project participants on a pro-rata basis. Allocation of credits should be agreed among the project participants.

8.6.2 Issuance of the Credits

After receiving the JCM Credits Issuance Request Form and accompanying documents, the secretariat reviews the completeness of the documents and notifies the project participants and the TPE of the result within 7 calendar days. Upon positive conclusion of the completeness check, the Joint Committee makes the final decision on whether to notify the governments of Japan and the host country of the amount of credits to be issued. The secretariat notifies each government, the project participants, and the TPE of the Joint Committee's decision.

After receiving the notification from the secretariat, each government issues the corresponding amount of credits specified in the notification to the respective accounts of the project participants in the registry. Each side then notifies the Joint Committee through the secretariat regarding the issuance of credits. The secretariat archives all the information regarding the issuance of credits and makes them publicly available through the JCM website.

Figure 8.2 shows the flow of the issuance process, including cases of negative outcome of the completeness check and Joint Committee decision.

---

[49]   Japan JCM registry. https://www.jcmregistry.go.jp/
       Indonesia JCM registry. http://jcm.ekon.go.id/en/index.php/content/OTE%253D/information_on_registry

Figure 8.2: Flowchart of the Credit Issuance Process

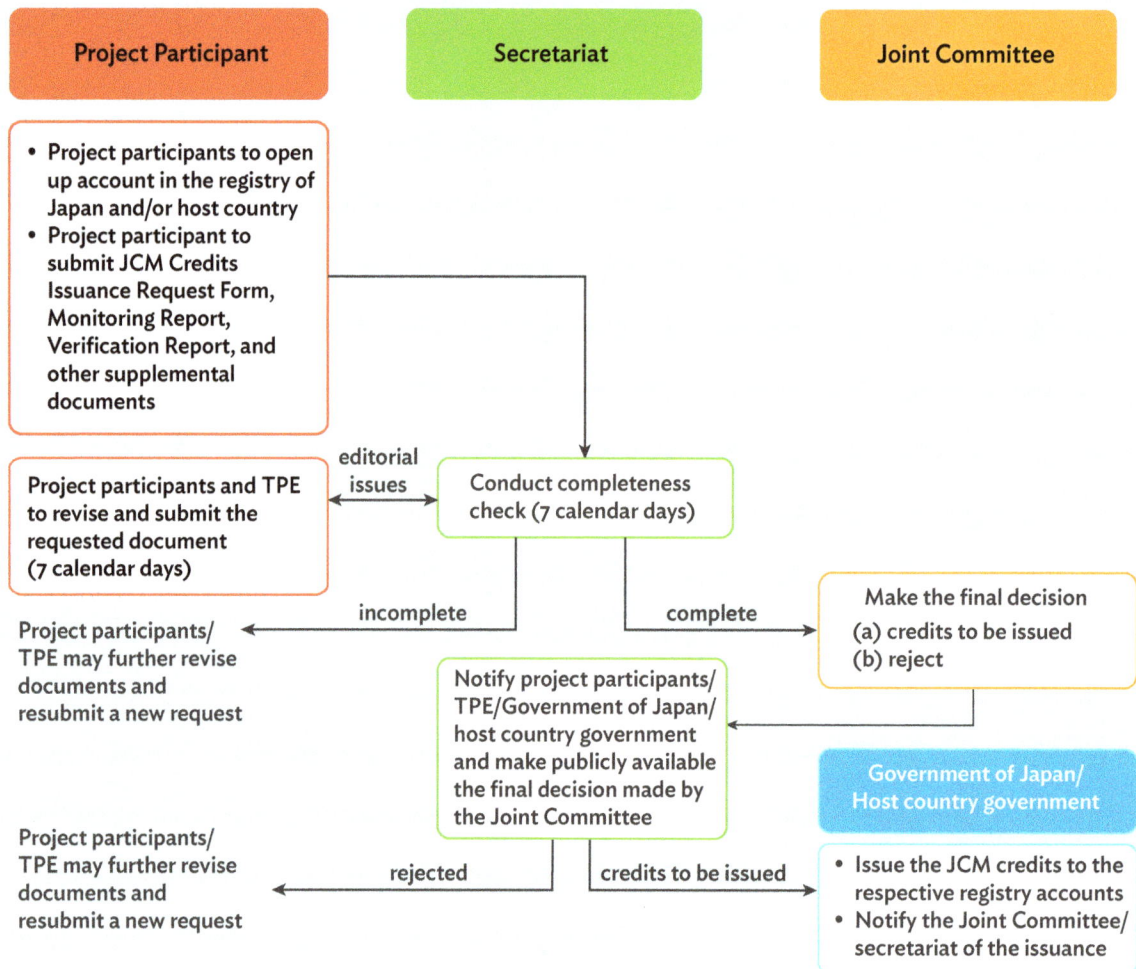

Project Participant	Secretariat	Joint Committee

- Project participants to open up account in the registry of Japan and/or host country
- Project participant to submit JCM Credits Issuance Request Form, Monitoring Report, Verification Report, and other supplemental documents

Project participants and TPE to revise and submit the requested document (7 calendar days)

editorial issues

Conduct completeness check (7 calendar days)

Project participants/ TPE may further revise documents and resubmit a new request

incomplete

complete

Make the final decision
(a) credits to be issued
(b) reject

Notify project participants/ TPE/Government of Japan/ host country government and make publicly available the final decision made by the Joint Committee

Government of Japan/ Host country government

Project participants/ TPE may further revise documents and resubmit a new request

rejected

credits to be issued

- Issue the JCM credits to the respective registry accounts
- Notify the Joint Committee/ secretariat of the issuance

JCM = Joint Crediting Mechanism, TPE = third-party entity.

Source: Authors

MODULE 9:
POST-REGISTRATION PROJECT CHANGES

9.1 INTRODUCTION TO THE MODULE

The objective of this module is to provide project participants with information on how to apply for a post-registration change. This module is divided into four subsections: (9.1) Introduction to the Module, (9.2) What Is a Post-Registration Project Change, (9.3) Procedure for Obtaining Approval for Temporary and Permanent Changes, and (9.4) Changes to the Modalities of Communication Statement.

9.2 WHAT IS A POST-REGISTRATION PROJECT CHANGE?

A project change refers to when the implemented project differs from what was described in the registered project design document (PDD) and/or methodology. Project changes are classified into the following three types:[50]

(a)   changes determined by the third-party entity (TPE) that do not prevent the use of the applied methodology,

(b)   changes identified by the project participants prior to verification or by the TPE during verification that would prevent the use of the applied methodology, or

(c)   changes identified by the project participants or determined by the TPE that prevent the use of the applied methodology.

The above types of changes apply to both temporary and permanent changes made during the course of implementing the project in reference to the registered PDD and/or methodology. If the project participants identify any post registration project change prior to verification, or by the TPE during verification, the project participants need to address those changes identified in order to continue and to have credits issued.

---

[50]   For Indonesian projects, the Joint Crediting Mechanism Project Cycle Procedure provides a detailed explanation of the process to follow if project changes are required on the sustainable development implementation plan.

9.3 PROCEDURE FOR OBTAINING APPROVAL FOR TEMPORARY AND PERMANENT CHANGES

Type (a): If the changes determined by the TPE do not prevent the use of the applied methodology, the project participants need to revise the PDD and submit it to the secretariat prior to the first issuance request.

Type (b): If the changes identified by the project participants prior to verification or by the TPE during verification *may* prevent the use of the applied methodology, the project participants need to request approval from the Joint Committee regarding the changes, prior to the submission of the request for issuance of credits. This is done by submitting a completed Post-Registration Changes Request Form and a revised PDD to the secretariat.

The secretariat prepares and maintains a publicly available list of all submitted requests for approval of changes through the JCM website. Upon receipt of the request for approval of changes, the secretariat conducts within 7 calendar days the completeness check to determine whether the request for approval of changes is complete. After the positive conclusion of the completeness check, the secretariat, within 14 calendar days, prepares and sends to the co-chairs of the Joint Committee a summary note on the request with a recommendation on the course of action, or with a notification that the case will be considered by the Joint Committee. During this period, the secretary may request project participants to submit revised documents and/or information, or seek guidance from relevant experts.

Once the summary note is confirmed by the co-chairs and distributed to the Joint Committee, the Joint Committee decides whether to approve the request. If it is approved, the secretariat makes the revised PDD publicly available on the JCM website as the registered PDD, and this version is applied for future requests for issuance.

Type (c): If the changes identified by the project participants or determined by the TPE *definitively* prevent the use of the applied methodology, the project participants shall withdraw the project. The project participants may resubmit a request for registration with a new PDD (based on a new methodology) for the withdrawn project.

The process is illustrated in Figure 9.1.

Figure 9.1: Flowchart of the Post-Registration Change Approval Process

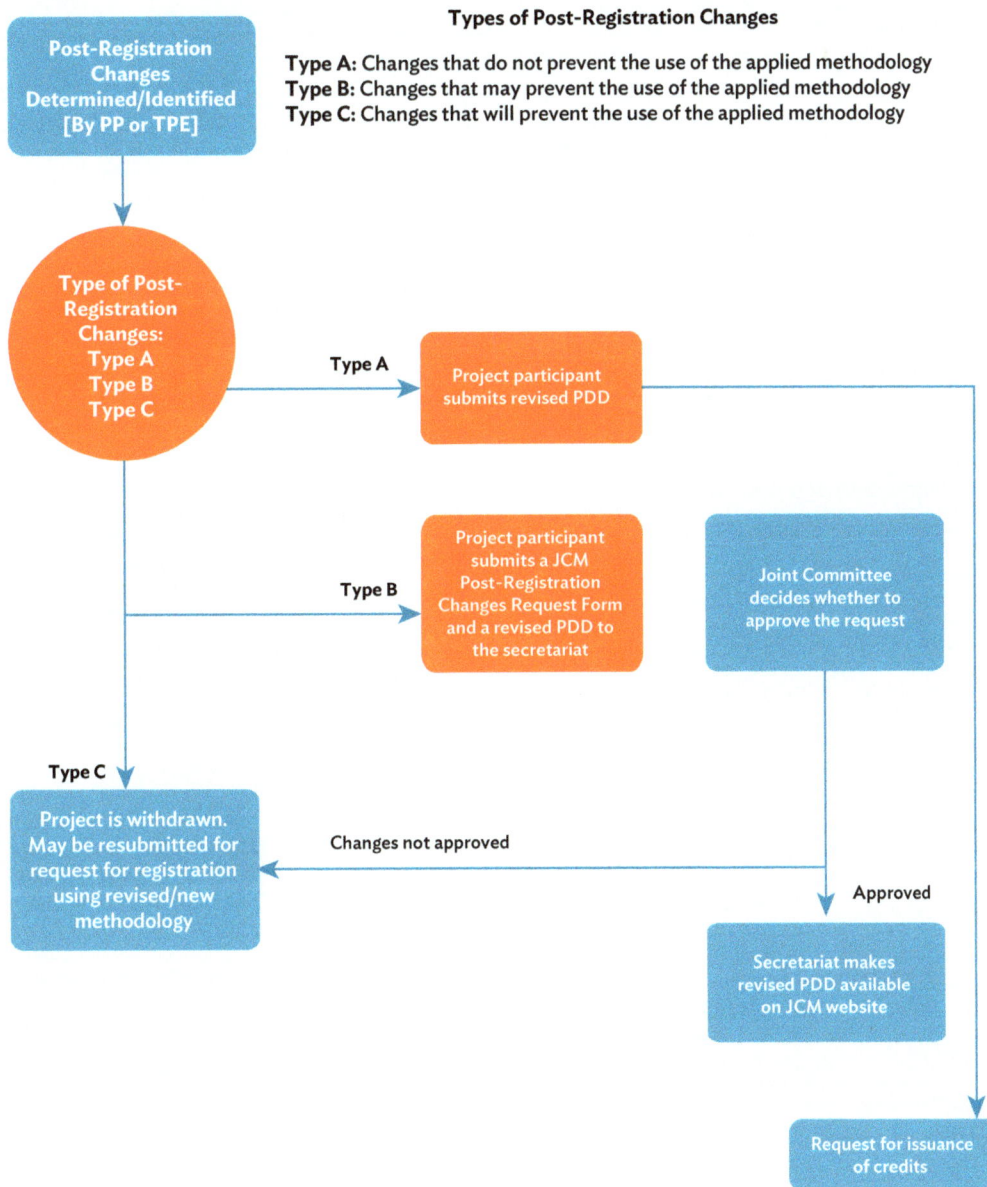

Types of Post-Registration Changes

Type A: Changes that do not prevent the use of the applied methodology
Type B: Changes that may prevent the use of the applied methodology
Type C: Changes that will prevent the use of the applied methodology

```
Post-Registration Changes Determined/Identified [By PP or TPE]
        │
        ▼
Type of Post-Registration Changes: Type A Type B Type C
        │
        ├── Type A ──▶ Project participant submits revised PDD
        │
        ├── Type B ──▶ Project participant submits a JCM Post-Registration Changes Request Form and a revised PDD to the secretariat
        │                                      Joint Committee decides whether to approve the request
        │
        └── Type C ──▶ Project is withdrawn. May be resubmitted for request for registration using revised/new methodology

Changes not approved

Approved ──▶ Secretariat makes revised PDD available on JCM website

Request for issuance of credits
```

JCM = Joint Crediting Mechanism, PDD = project design document, PP = project participant, TPE = third-party entity.
Source: Authors.

9.4 CHANGES TO THE MODALITIES OF COMMUNICATION STATEMENT

Project participants may need to change the modalities of communication statement (MOC). This could include changes regarding project participants or a change in the designated focal point. To do this, project participants, can submit a JCM Modalities of Communication Statement Form to the secretariat.

9.4.1 Changes to the project participants

To make any changes to the project participants' information in the MOC the focal point(s) may submit Annex 1 of the JCM Modalities of Communication Statement Form to the secretariat. Change to the project participants include:

(i)   addition of a project participant;

(ii)   changes related to entity name or legal status;

(iii) withdrawal of a project participant (if a project participant has ceased operations and is unable to sign the JCM Modalities of Communication Statement Form, the submission is accompanied by documented evidence of the cessation); and

(iv)   changes related only to contact details and specimen signatures.

9.4.2 Changes to the focal point

To change the focal point entity, for any reason and at any time, the project participants for a registered JCM project must submit a new JCM Modalities of Communication Statement Form signed by all project participants, either through the focal point(s) or any of the project participants directly.

The JCM Modalities of Communication Statement Form should be submitted along with supporting documentation, such as powers of attorney, extracts from board meeting minutes, company association documentation, or extracts or certificates from national company registries. If such documentation cannot be verified online, it should be dated or notarized within 2 years from the time of the submission of a request for a change to an established MOC.

APPENDIX 1:
LIST OF REGISTERED JOINT CREDITING MECHANISM PROJECTS

Registration Date	Host Country	Project Title	Emission Reduction*
3 Jun 2016	Indonesia	Installation of Inverter-Type Air Conditioning System, LED Lighting and Separate Type Fridge Freezer Showcase to Grocery Stores in Republic of Indonesia	115 tCO_2e
24 Mar 2016	Indonesia	Energy Saving for Air-Conditioning at Textile Factory by Introducing High-Efficiency Centrifugal Chiller in Batang, Central Java (Phase 2)	145 tCO_2e
24 Mar 2016	Indonesia	Energy Saving for Air-Conditioning at Textile Factory by Introducing High-Efficiency Centrifugal Chiller in Karawang, West Java	176 tCO_2e
29 Mar 2015	Indonesia	Project of Introducing High-Efficiency Refrigerator to a Food Industry Cold Storage in Indonesia	120 tCO_2e
29 Mar 2015	Indonesia	Project of Introducing High-Efficiency Refrigerator to a Frozen Food Processing Plant in Indonesia	21 tCO_2e
31 Oct 2014	Indonesia	Energy Saving for Air Conditioning and Process Cooling by Introducing High-Efficiency Centrifugal Chiller	114 tCO_2e
30 Jun 2015	Mongolia	Installation of High-Efficiency Heat Only Boilers in 118th School of Ulaanbaatar City Project	92 tCO_2e
30 Jun 2015	Mongolia	Centralization of Heat Supply System by Installation of High-Efficiency Heat Only Boilers in Bornuur Soum Project	206 tCO_2e
12 Jul 2016	Palau	Small Scale Solar Power Plants for Commercial Facilities in Island States II	315 tCO_2e
12 Jul 2016	Palau	Small Scale Solar Power Plants for Schools in Island States	108 tCO_2e
21 April 2015	Palau	Small Scale Solar Power Plants for Commercial Facilities in Island States	227 tCO_2e
15 May 2016	Viet Nam	Introduction of Amorphous High-Efficiency Transformers in Power Distribution Systems in the Southern Part of Viet Nam	610 tCO_2e
15 May 2016	Viet Nam	Low Carbon Hotel Project in Viet Nam: Improving the Energy Efficiency of Commercial Buildings by Utilization of High-Efficiency Equipment	272 tCO_2e
30 Nov 15	Viet Nam	Promotion of Green Hospitals by Improving Efficiency/ Environment in National Hospitals in Viet Nam	515 tCO_2e
04 Aug 2015	Viet Nam	Eco-Driving by Utilizing Digital Tachograph System	296 tCO_2e

tCO_2e = tons of carbon dioxide equivalent.

* Estimated average emission reductions per annum.

Source: The Joint Crediting Mechanism. Accessed on 15 September 2016 at https://www.jcm.go.jp/

APPENDIX 2:
LIST OF APPROVED METHODOLOGIES

Host Country	Methodology	Methodology Type	Number of Successfully Registered Projects
Bangladesh	**BD_AM001:** Energy saving by introduction of high-efficiency centrifugal chiller	Energy demand	0
Cambodia	**KH_AM001:** Installation of LED street lighting system with wireless network control	Energy demand	0
Ethiopia	**ET_AM001:** Electrification of communities using micro hydropower generation	Energy industries	0
Indonesia	**ID_AM001:** Power generation by waste heat recovery in cement industry	Energy industries	0
Indonesia	**ID_AM002:** Energy saving by introduction of high-efficiency centrifugal chiller	Energy demand	3
Indonesia	**ID_AM003:** Installation of energy-efficient refrigerators using natural refrigerant at food industry cold storage and frozen food processing plant	Energy demand	2
Indonesia	**ID_AM004:** Installation of inverter-type air conditioning system for cooling for grocery store	Energy demand	1
Indonesia	**ID_AM005:** Installation of LED lighting for grocery store	Energy demand	1
Indonesia	**ID_AM006:** GHG emission reductions through optimization of refinery plant operation in Indonesia	Energy demand	0
Indonesia	**ID_AM007:** GHG emission reductions through optimization of boiler operation in Indonesia	Energy demand	0
Indonesia	**ID_AM008:** Installation of a separate type fridge-freezer showcase by using natural refrigerant for grocery store to reduce air conditioning load inside the store	Energy demand	1
Indonesia	**ID_AM009:** Replacement of conventional burners with regenerative burners for aluminum holding furnaces	Energy demand	0
Indonesia	**ID_AM010:** Introducing double-bundle modular electric heat pumps to a new building	Energy demand	0
Kenya	**KE_AM001:** Electrification of communities using micro hydropower generation	Energy industries	0
Maldives	**MV_AM001:** Displacement of grid and captive genset electricity by solar PV system	Energy industries	0
Mongolia	**MN_AM001:** Installation of energy-saving transmission lines in the Mongolian grid	Energy distribution	0
Mongolia	**MN_AM002:** Replacement and installation of high-efficiency heat only boiler (HOB) for hot water supply systems	Energy industries	2

continued on next page

Table *continued*

Host Country	Methodology	Methodology Type	Number of Successfully Registered Projects
Palau	**PW_AM001:** Displacement of Grid and captive genset electricity by a small-scale solar PV system	Energy industries	3
Thailand	**TH_AM001:** Installation of Solar PV System	Energy industries	0
Thailand	**TH_AM002:** Energy Saving by Introduction of Multi-stage Oil-Free Air Compressor	Energy demand	0
Viet Nam	**VN_AM001:** Transportation energy-efficiency activities by installing digital tachograph systems	Transport	1
Viet Nam	**VN_AM002:** Introduction of room air conditioners equipped with inverters	Energy demand	1
Viet Nam	**VN_AM003:** Improving the energy efficiency of commercial buildings by utilization of high efficiency equipment	Energy demand	1
Viet Nam	**VN_AM004:** Anaerobic digestion of organic waste for biogas utilization within wholesale markets	Waste handling and disposal	0
Viet Nam	**VN_AM005:** Installation of energy-efficient transformers in a power distribution grid	Energy distribution	1

GHG = greenhouse gas, PV = photovoltaic.

Source: The Joint Crediting Mechanism. Accessed on 15 September 2016 at https://www.jcm.go.jp/

APPENDIX 3:

LIST OF JOINT CREDITING MECHANISM MODEL AND DEMONSTRATION PROJECTS SELECTED FOR SUPPORT BY THE GOVERNMENT OF JAPAN

Country	Title	Fiscal Year	Agency	Entity
Bangladesh	Energy Saving of Air Conditioning System by Recovering Waste Heat from Engine in Textile Factory	FY2016	MOE	Ebara Refrigeration Equipment & Systems
Bangladesh	50MW Solar PV Power Plant Project	FY2015	MOE	Pacific Consultants
Bangladesh	Installation of High Efficiency Centrifugal Chiller for Air Conditioning System in Clothing Tag Factory	FY2015	MOE	Ebara Refrigeration Equipment & Systems
Bangladesh	Installation of High Efficiency Loom at Weaving Factory	FY2015	MOE	Toyota Tsusho
Bangladesh	Introduction of PV–Diesel Hybrid System at Fastening Manufacturing Plant	FY2015	MOE	YKK
Bangladesh	Energy Saving for Air Conditioning & Facility Cooling by High Efficiency Centrifugal Chiller (Suburbs of Dhaka)	FY2014	MOE	Ebara Refrigeration Equipment & Systems
Cambodia	Introduction of 0.8MW Solar Power Generation in International School	FY2016	MOE	Asian Gateway
Cambodia	Introduction of 1MW Solar Power System and High Efficiency Centrifugal Chiller in Large Shopping Mall	FY2016	MOE	Aeon Mall
Cambodia	Introduction of High Efficiency LED Lighting Utilizing Wireless Network	FY2015	MOE	Minebea
Cambodia	Small-Scale Biomass Power Generation by Using Stirling Engines	FY2013	MOE	Promaterials
Costa Rica	Introduction of the High Efficiency Chiller and the Exhaust Heat Recovery System	FY2016	MOE	NTT DATA Institute of Management Consulting
Costa Rica	5MW Solar Power Project in Belen	FY2016	MOE	NTT DATA Institute of Management Consulting
Ethiopia	Introduction of Biomass CHP Plant in Flooring Factory	FY2015	MOE	Pacific Consultants
Indonesia	Energy Saving in Industrial Wastewater Treatment System for Rubber Industry	FY2016	MOE	Environmental Management & Technology Center

continued on next page

Table *continued*

Country	Title	Fiscal Year	Agency	Entity
Indonesia	Energy Saving for Air Conditioning Utility System in the Airport Terminal by High Efficiency Operating System	FY2016	MOE	iFORCOM Tokyo
Indonesia	Introduction of High Efficiency Looms in Weaving Mill	FY2016	MOE	Nisshinbo Textile
Indonesia	Introduction of LED Lighting to Sales Stores	FY2016	MOE	Fast Retailing
Indonesia	10MW Mini Hydro Power Plant Project in North Sumatra	FY2016	MOE	Toyo Energy Farm
Indonesia	REDD+ Project in Boalemo District	FY2016	MOE	Kanematsu
Indonesia	Energy Saving by Utilizing Waste Heat at Hotel	FY2015	MOE	Takasago Thermal Engineering
Indonesia	Energy Saving for Air Conditioning at Shopping Mall with High Efficiency Centrifugal Chiller	FY2015	MOE	NTT Facilities
Indonesia	Energy Saving for Industrial Park with Smart LED Street Lighting System	FY2015	MOE	NTT Facilities
Indonesia	Energy Saving for Office Building with High Efficiency Water Cooled Air-Conditioning Unit	FY2015	MOE	NTT Facilities
Indonesia	Installation of Cogeneration System in Hotel	FY2015	MOE	NTT DATA Institute of Management Consulting
Indonesia	Installation of Gas Co-Generation System for Automobile Manufacturing Plant	FY2015	MOE	Toyota Tsusho
Indonesia	Introduction of High Efficiency Once-Through Boiler System in Film Factory	FY2015	MOE	Mitsubishi Plastics
Indonesia	REDD+ Project in Boalemo District	FY2015	MOE	Kanematsu
Indonesia	Energy Saving for Textile Factory Facility Cooling by High-Efficiency Centrifugal Chiller	FY2014	MOE	Ebara Refrigeration Equipment & Systems
Indonesia	Energy Saving through Introduction of Regenerative Burners to the Aluminum Holding Furnace of the Automotive Components Manufacturer	FY2014	MOE	Toyotsu Machinery/Hokuriku Techno
Indonesia	Introduction of High Efficient Old Corrugated Cartons Process at Paper Factory	FY2014	MOE	Kanematsu
Indonesia	Power Generation by Waste Heat Recovery in Cement Industry	FY2014	MOE	JFE Engineering
Indonesia	Reducing Greenhouse Gas Emission at Textile Factories by Upgrading to Air-Saving Loom	FY2014	MOE	Toray Industries
Indonesia	Solar Power Hybrid System Installation to Existing Base Transceiver Stations in Off-Grid Area	FY2014	MOE	Telekomunikasi Selular
Indonesia	Energy Saving by Optimum Operation at Oil Factory	FY2013	METI/NEDO	Yokogawa Solution Service
Indonesia	Thin-Film Solar Power Plant	FY2013	METI/NEDO	Sharp
Indonesia	Utility Facility Operation Optimization Technology into Oil Factory	FY2013	METI/NEDO	Azbil
Indonesia	Energy Efficient Refrigerants to Cold Chain Industry	FY2013	MOE	Mayekawa Mfg.
Indonesia	Energy Saving by Installation of Double Bundle-Type Heat Pump	FY2013	MOE	Toyota Tsusho

continued on next page

Table *continued*

Country	Title	Fiscal Year	Agency	Entity
Indonesia	Energy Saving for Air Conditioning at Textile Factory	FY2013	MOE	Ebara Refrigeration Equipment & Systems
Indonesia	Energy Saving for Air Conditioning and Process Cooling at Factory	FY2013	MOE	Ebara Refrigeration Equipment & Systems
Indonesia	Energy Savings at Convenience Stores	FY2013	MOE	Lawson
Kenya	6MW Small Hydropower Generation Project in Rupingazi	FY2015	MOE	Pacific Consultants
Kenya	Introduction of Solar PV System at Salt Factory	FY2015	MOE	Pacific Consultants.
Kenya	Solar Diesel Abatement Project	FY2014	MOE	Ingerosec
Lao PDR	REDD+ Project in Luang Prabang Province through Controlling Slash-and-Burn	FY2016	MOE	Waseda University
Lao PDR	REDD+ Project in Luang Prabang Province through Controlling Slash-and-Burn	FY2015	MOE	Waseda University
Lao PDR	Energy Efficiency Container Data Center	FY2014	METI/ NEDO	Toyota Tsusho, Internet Initiative Japan/Mitsubishi UFJ Morgan Stanley Securities
Malaysia	PV Power Generation System for the Office Building	FY2014	MOE	NTT DATA Institute of Management Consulting
Maldives	School Building Rooftop Solar Power Plant Project	FY2014	MOE	Pacific Consultants/InterAct
Mexico	Introduction of 4.8MW Power Generation with Methane Gas Recovery System	FY2016	MOE	NTT DATA Institute of Management Consulting
Mexico	Domo de San Pedro II Geothermal Power Generation	FY2015	MOE	Mitsubishi Hitachi Power Systems
Mexico	Energy Saving by Converting from Hg-Cell Process to Ion-Exchange Membrane Process at Chlorine Production Plant	FY2015	MOE	ThyssenKrupp Uhde Chlorine Engineers (Japan)
Mongolia	Installation of 8.3MW Solar Power Plant in Ulaanbaatar Suburb Farm	FY2016	MOE	Farmdo
Mongolia	10MW Solar Power Project in Darkhan City	FY2015	MOE	Sharp
Mongolia	Installation of 2.1MW Solar Power Plant for Power Supply in Ulaanbaatar Suburb	FY2015	MOE	Farmdo
Mongolia	High Efficiency and Low Loss Power Transmission and Distribution System	FY2013	METI/ NEDO	Hitachi
Mongolia	Upgrading and Installation of Centralized Control System of High-Efficiency Heat Only Boiler (HOB)	FY2013	MOE	Suuri-Keikaku
Myanmar	Introduction of High-efficiency Once-through Boiler in Instant Noodle Factory	FY2016	MOE	Acecook
Myanmar	Introduction of Energy Saving Brewing Systems to Beer Factory	FY2016	MOE	Kirin Holdings
Myanmar	Introduction of Waste to Energy Plant in Yangon City	FY2015	MOE	JFE Engineering
Palau	Small-Scale Solar Power Plants for Commercial Facilities Project II	FY2014	MOE	Pacific Consultants
Palau	Solar PV System for Schools Project	FY2014	MOE	Pacific Consultants

continued on next page

Table *continued*

Country	Title	Fiscal Year	Agency	Entity
Palau	Small-Scale Solar Power Plant for Commercial Facilities in Island States	FY2013	MOE	Pacific Consultants
Saudi Arabia	Introduction of High Efficiency Electrolyzer in Chlorine Production Plant	FY2015	MOE	Kanematsu
Thailand	Introduction of Energy Efficient Refrigeration System in Industrial Cold Storage	FY2016	MOE	Kanematsu
Thailand	Introduction of 1.5MW Rooftop Solar Power System and Advanced EMS for Power Supply in Paint Factory	FY2016	MOE	Finetech
Thailand	Introduction of 3.4MW Rooftop Solar Power System to Air Conditioning Parts Factories	FY2016	MOE	Sharp
Thailand	Introduction of Energy Saving Refrigerator and Evaporator with Mechanical Vapor Recompression in Amino Acid Producing Plant	FY2016	MOE	Kyowa Hakko Bio
Thailand	Introduction of Cogeneration System to Motor Parts Factory	FY2016	MOE	Denso
Thailand	Introduction of 12MW Power Generation System by Waste Heat Recovery for Cement Plant	FY2016	MOE	NTT DATA Institute of Management Consulting
Thailand	Introduction of High Efficiency Chilled Water Supply System in Milk Factory	FY2016	MOE	Tepia Corporation Japan
Thailand	Introduction of LED Lighting to Sales Stores	FY2016	MOE	Fast Retailing
Thailand	Introduction of High Efficiency Ion Exchange Membrane Electrolyzer in Caustic Soda Production Plant	FY2016	MOE	Asahi Glass
Thailand	Energy Saving at Convenience Stores with High Efficiency Air Conditioning and Refrigerated Showcase	FY2015	MOE	FamilyMart
Thailand	Energy Saving for Air Conditioning in Tire Manufacturing Factory with High Efficiency Centrifugal Chiller	FY2015	MOE	Inabata & Co.
Thailand	Energy Saving for Semiconductor Factory with High Efficiency Centrifugal Chiller and Compressor	FY2015	MOE	Sony Semiconductor
Thailand	Installation of Co-Generation Plant for On-Site Energy Supply in Motorcycle Factory	FY2015	MOE	Nippon Steel & Sumikin Engineering
Thailand	Installation of High Efficiency Air Conditioning System and Chillers in Semiconductor Factory	FY2015	MOE	Sony Semiconductor
Thailand	Introduction of Solar PV System on Factory Rooftop	FY2015	MOE	Pacific Consultants
Thailand	Reducing Greenhouse Gas Emission at Textile Factory by Upgrading to Air-Saving Loom (Samutprakarn)	FY2015	MOE	Toray Industries
Viet Nam	Introduction of Energy Saving Equipment to Automotive Wire Production Factory	FY2016	MOE	Yazaki Parts
Viet Nam	Introduction of Amorphous High Efficiency Transformer in Northern, Central, and Southern Power Grids	FY2016	MOE	Yuko Keiso

continued on next page

Table *continued*

Country	Title	Fiscal Year	Agency	Entity
Viet Nam	Installation of Energy Saving Equipment in Lens Factory	FY2016	MOE	Hoya
Viet Nam	Introduction of High Efficiency Water Pumps in Da Nang City	FY2016	MOE	Yokohama Water
Viet Nam	Introduction of 4.75MW Power Generation System by Waste Heat Recovery for Cement Plant	FY2016	MOE	NTT DATA Institute of Management Consulting
Viet Nam	Energy Saving and Work Efficiency Improvement Project by Special LED Equipment with New Technology, COB	FY2015	METI/ NEDO	Stanley Electric
Viet Nam	Energy Saving in Acid Lead Battery Factory with Container Formation Facility	FY2015	MOE	Hitachi Chemical
Viet Nam	Energy Saving in Factories with Air Conditioning Control System	FY2015	MOE	Yuko Keiso
Viet Nam	Energy Saving in Lens Factory with Energy Efficient Air Conditioners	FY2015	MOE	Ricoh
Viet Nam	Installation of High Efficiency Kiln in Sanitary Ware Manufacturing Factory	FY2015	MOE	TOTO
Viet Nam	Introduction of Amorphous High Efficiency Transformers in Southern and Central Power Grids	FY2015	MOE	Yuko Keiso
Viet Nam	Energy Saving in Acid Lead Battery Factory with Container Formation Facility	FY2015	MOE	Hitachi Chemical
Viet Nam	Energy Saving in Lens Factory with Energy Efficient Air Conditioners	FY2015	MOE	Ricoh
Viet Nam	Introduction of High Efficiency Air Conditioning in Hotel	FY2015	MOE	NTT DATA Institute of Management Consulting
Viet Nam	Energy Efficient Paper Making Process	FY2014	METI/ NEDO	Marubeni/Nomura Research Institute
Viet Nam	Anaerobic Digestion of Organic Waste for Biogas Utilization at Market	FY2014	MOE	Hitachi Zosen/K.K. Satisfactory International
Viet Nam	Eco-Driving by Utilizing Digital Tachograph System	FY2014	MOE	Nippon Express
Viet Nam	Introduction of Amorphous High Efficiency Transformers in Power Distribution Systems	FY2014	MOE	Yuko Keiso
Viet Nam	Energy Saving by BEMS Optimum Operation at Hotel	FY2013	METI/ NEDO	Hibiya Engineering/ Mitsubishi UFJ Morgan Stanley Securities
Viet Nam	Energy Saving by Inverter Air Conditioner Optimum Operation at National Hospital	FY2013	METI/ NEDO	Mitsubishi Electric / Mitsubishi Corporation/ Mitsubishi UFJ Morgan Stanley Securities

BEMS = building energy management system, COB = chip on board, FY = fiscal year, Lao PDR = Lao People's Democratic Republic, LED = light emitting diode, METI = Ministry of Economy, Trade and Industry of Japan, MOE = Ministry of the Environment Japan, MW = megawatt, NEDO = New Energy and Industrial Technology Development Organization, PV = photovoltaic, REDD+ = Reducing emissions from deforestation and forest degradation and the role of conservation, sustainable management of forests and enhancement of forest carbon stocks in developing countries.

Source: List of Selected Projects and Studies under JCM Support Programme of the New Mechanisms Information Platform (www.mmechanisms. org/e/support/adoption.html).

JCM_ID_AM003_ver01.0
Sectoral scope: 03

Joint Crediting Mechanism Approved Methodology ID_AM003
"Installation of Energy-efficient Refrigerators Using Natural Refrigerant at Food Industry Cold Storage and Frozen Food Processing Plant"

A. Title of the methodology

Installation of Energy-efficient Refrigerators Using Natural Refrigerant at Food Industry Cold Storage and Frozen Food Processing Plant

B. Terms and definitions

Terms	Definitions
Two stage compressor	A two stage compressor is a compressor equipped with a low stage compressor and a high stage compressor between an evaporator and a condenser which increases the pressure of low pressure refrigerant gas from the evaporator up to the intermediate pressure using the low stage compressor and further increases the pressure of the refrigerant gas using the high stage compressor to feed it to the condenser.
Secondary loop cooling system	A secondary loop cooling system is an indirect cooling system that cools the object with a secondary refrigerant (e.g., brine) which is cooled by a primary refrigerant. The secondary loop cooling system primarily consists of the refrigerator which is mainly composed of the compressor and heat exchangers as the primary refrigeration cycle and pumps, heat exchangers and fans as the secondary refrigeration cycle. The secondary loop cooling system is described as "primary refrigerant/secondary refrigerant" (e.g., "HFC/brine").
Coefficient of Performance (COP)	COP is defined as a value calculated by dividing refrigeration capacity by electricity consumption of a refrigerator under a full load condition. Electricity consumption of a refrigerator is defined in this methodology as the electricity used to operate the compressor. Electricity consumption of pumps for circulating the secondary refrigerant, and other ancillary

I-1

	equipments are not included in the COP calculation.
	The temperature conditions at which COPs are calculated in this methodology are shown below:
	\<For cold storage\>
	Note : Temperature condition: - 25 deg. C
	Cooling water fed to condenser: inlet 32 deg. C
	\<For individual quick freezer\>
	Note : Temperature condition: - 35 deg. C
	Cooling water fed to condenser: inlet 32 deg. C
	Individual quick freezer is used for the purpose of continuous freezing for food products fed by a belt conveyor system.
Natural refrigerant	Natural refrigerant refers to naturally occurring substances with refrigeration capacity and with zero ozone depletion potential (ODP) (e.g., CO_2 and NH_3).
Periodical check	Periodical check is a periodical maintenance operation done by the manufacturer or an agent who is authorized by the manufacturer to maintain refrigerator performance (not including part replacement or overhaul).

C. Summary of the methodology

Items	Summary
GHG emission reduction measures	This methodology applies to projects that aim to save energy by introducing high efficiency refrigerators to the food industry cold storage and frozen food processing plants in Indonesia.
Calculation of reference emissions	Reference emissions are GHG emissions from the usage of reference refrigerators, calculated by using data of power consumption of project refrigerator, ratio of COPs of reference/project refrigerators and CO_2 emission factor for electricity consumed.
Calculation of project emissions	Project emissions are GHG emissions from the usage of project refrigerator, calculated with power consumption of project refrigerator and CO_2 emission factor for electricity consumed.
Monitoring parameters	● Amount of electricity consumed by project refrigerator

JCM_ID_AM003_ver01.0
Sectoral scope: 03

	• Electricity imported from the grid, where applicable • Operating time of captive electricity generator, where applicable

D. Eligibility criteria

This methodology is applicable to projects that satisfy all of the following criteria.

Criterion 1	The project installs cooling system at food industry cold storage and frozen food processing plants for the purpose of chilling the food products to below -20 deg. C.
Criterion 2	The project system is a secondary loop cooling system using natural refrigerant. CO_2 is used as the secondary refrigerant in the system.
Criterion 3	The refrigerator applied in the project cooling system is a two stage compressor refrigerator with a cooling capacity as shown below: For cold storage: less than 340kW For individual quick freezer: less than 260kW
Criterion 4	The compressor of the project refrigerator is controlled by inverter.
Criterion 5	COP of the project refrigerator i ($COP_{PJ,i}$) is shown below: For cold storage: more than 2.0 For individual quick freezer: more than 1.5
Criterion 6	Periodical check at least once a year is planned.
Criterion 7	Plan for not releasing the primary refrigerant used for project refrigerator is prepared. In the case of replacing the existing refrigerator with the project refrigerator, refrigerant used for the existing refrigerator is not released to the air.

E. Emission Sources and GHG types

Reference emissions	
Emission sources	GHG types
Electricity consumption by the reference refrigerator	CO_2
Project emissions	
Emission sources	GHG types
Electricity consumption by the project refrigerator	CO_2

F. Establishment and calculation of reference emissions

F.1. Establishment of reference emissions

Reference emissions are calculated by multiplying the power consumption of project refrigerator, ratio of COPs for reference/project refrigerators and CO_2 emission factor for electricity consumed.

Four types of cooling system are identified as possible cooling systems except for the project system: HFC dry expansion (single loop), NH_3 flooded, pump system (single loop), HFC/brine (secondary loop) and NH_3/brine (secondary loop). This methodology ensures that a net emission reduction is achieved by applying the following conservative assumptions:

• COP_{RE} value adopted:

The maximum COP values of refrigerators among the available data of the possible type cooling systems within the range specified by Criterion 2 is defined as COP_{RE} (1.71 for cold storage, 1.32 for individual quick freezer). The most common COP values lie between 1.60 and 1.65 for cold storages and between 1.20 and 1.25 for individual quick freezers.

• Electricity consumption of the pump for the secondary refrigerant:

Among the possible types of refrigerators, two possible cooling systems that use the secondary loop consume more electricity since the brine pump consumes more electricity than the CO_2 pump in the project cooling system. However, emissions from electricity consumption by the pump are not included in the emission calculations. The other two possible cooling systems using single loop have pumps that require almost equal amount of electricity to the project cooling system.

• Emissions associated with refrigerant loss from refrigerator:

Among the four possible types of cooling systems, two cooling systems use HFCs (R404A, R507A) as refrigerant and these have high GWP (3,000-4,000). The project cooling system uses a natural refrigerant that has a very small GWP (CO_2: 1, NH_3: less than 1). Emissions associated with the loss of refrigerant are not counted in the emission reduction calculation.

• Project refrigerator equipped with inverter:

The project refrigerator is controlled by inverter (as specified by Criterion 4). In this methodology, COP is defined under the condition of full load although in reality a cold storage is often operated under the condition of partial load where the efficiency of the refrigerator without inverter tends to decrease because of its intermittent operation. Although it is not clear

JCM_ID_AM003_ver01.0
Sectoral scope: 03

whether all the refrigerators of the four possible types of cooling systems are equipped with inverter, calculating emissions based on the COPs of full load conditions is deemed conservative since the efficiency of the project refrigerator is likely to be maintained either at the full load or at partial load condition as it is equipped with inverter.

F.2. Calculation of reference emissions

Reference emissions are calculated by the following equation.

$$RE_p = \sum_i \{ EC_{PJ,i,p} \times (COP_{PJ,i} \div COP_{RE,i}) \times EF_{elec} \}$$

RE_p	:	Reference emissions during the period p [tCO$_2$/p]
$EC_{PJ,i,p}$	:	Amount of electricity consumption of the project refrigerator i during the period p [MWh/p]
$COP_{PJ,i}$	:	COP of the project refrigerator type i
$COP_{RE,i}$	:	COP of the reference refrigerator type i
EF_{elec}	:	CO$_2$ emission factor for consumed electricity [tCO$_2$/MWh]

G. Calculation of project emissions

Project emissions are calculated by the following equation.

$$PE_p = \sum_i (EC_{PJ,i,p} \times EF_{elec})$$

PE_p	:	Project emissions during the period p [tCO$_2$/p]
$EC_{PJ,i,p}$	:	Amount of electricity consumption of the project refrigerator i during the period p [MWh/p]
EF_{elec}	:	CO$_2$ emission factor for consumed electricity [tCO$_2$/MWh]

H. Calculation of emissions reductions

Emissions reductions are calculated as the difference between the reference emissions and the project emissions, as follows:

$$ER_p = RE_p - PE_p$$

ER_p : Emissions Reductions during the period p [tCO$_2$/p]

RE_p : Reference Emissions during the period p [tCO$_2$/p]

PE_p : Project Emissions during the period p [tCO$_2$/p]

I. Data and parameters fixed *ex ante*

The source of each data and parameter fixed *ex ante* is listed as below.

Parameter	Description of data	Source
EF$_{elec}$	CO$_2$ emission factor for consumed electricity. When project refrigerator consumes only grid electricity or captive electricity, the project participant applies the CO$_2$ emission factor respectively. When project refrigerator may consume both grid electricity and captive electricity, the project participant applies the CO$_2$ emission factors for grid and captive electricity proportionately. Proportion of captive electricity is derived from dividing captive electricity generated by total electricity consumed at the project site. The total electricity consumed is a summation of grid electricity imported (EI$_{grid,p}$) and captive electricity generated (EG$_{gen,p}$)* during the monitoring period. * Captive electricity generated can be derived from metering electricity generated or monitored operating time (h$_{gen,p}$) and rated capacity of generator (RC$_{gen}$).	[Grid electricity] The most recent value available at the time of validation is applied and fixed for the monitoring period thereafter. The data is sourced from "Emission Factors of Electricity Interconnection Systems", National Committee on Clean Development Mechanism Indonesian DNA for CDM unless otherwise instructed by the Joint Committee. [Captive electricity] CDM approved small scale methodology: AMS-I.A.

JCM_ID_AM003_ver01.0
Sectoral scope: 03

	[CO$_2$ emission factor] For grid electricity: The most recent value available from the source stated in this table at the time of validation For captive electricity: 0.8* [tCO$_2$/MWh] *The most recent value available from CDM approved small scale methodology AMS-I.A. at the time of validation is applied.	
COP$_{RE,i}$	COP of the reference refrigerator *i*. The default values for COP$_{RE,i}$ are set as follows: For cold storage: 1.71 For individual quick freezer: 1.32	Specifications for the quotation or factory acceptance test data at the time of shipment by manufacturer. The default COP values are derived from the maximum value of COP among the available data of the possible types of refrigerators except project within the range specified by Criterion 2. The survey should prove the use of clear methodology. The COP$_{RE,i}$ should be revised if necessary from survey result which is conducted by JC or project participants every three years.
COP$_{PJ,i}$	COP of the project refrigerator *i*	Specifications for the quotation or factory acceptance test data at the time of shipment by manufacturer.
RC$_{gen}$	Rated capacity of generator, where applicable.	Specification of generator for captive electricity

History of the document

Version	Date	Contents revised
01.0	30 October 2014	JC3, Annex 5 Initial approval.

JCM_ID_F_PDD_ver01.0

JCM Project Design Document Form

A. Project description

A.1. Title of the JCM project

Project of Introducing High Efficiency Refrigerator to a Food Industry Cold Storage in Indonesia

A.2. General description of project and applied technologies and/or measures

The proposed JCM project aims to save energy by introducing a high efficiency refrigerator to a food industry cold storage in Indonesia. The project is expected to reduce 140 tCO_{2e} of greenhouse gas (GHG) emissions annually through installation of a refrigerator in a newly established food industry cold storage of PT Adib Global Food Supplies in West Java Province, Indonesia.

In line with the JCM approved methodology ID_AM003, reference emissions are calculated by multiplying electricity consumption of the project refrigerator (MWh), ratio of COPs (Coefficient Of Performance) for reference/project refrigerators and CO_2 emission factor for electricity consumed (tCO_{2e}/MWh), while project emissions are calculated by multiplying electricity consumption of the project refrigerator (MWh) and CO_2 emission factor for electricity consumed (tCO_{2e}/MWh).

COP of the project refrigerator (COP_{PJ}) is 2.2 which is calculated by dividing cooling capacity (189 kW*) of the refrigerator by its electricity consumption (86kW*) based on the manufacturer's catalogue. COP of reference refrigerator (COP_{RE}) is set as 1.71 which is the maximum value among the collected data for commercially available refrigerators in Indonesia to ensure a net emission reduction. Electricity consumption of the project refrigerator will be obtained by monitoring.

The estimated amount of annual electricity consumption by the project refrigerator is 603 MWh, while that of the reference refrigerator is 776 MWh, resulting in 22% of energy saving. The reference emissions are 631 tCO_{2e} and the project emissions are 491 tCO_{2e} resulting in an estimated annual GHG emission reduction of 140 tCO_{2e}.

*:Temperature condition: - 25 deg. C, Cooling water fed to condenser: inlet 32 deg. C

A.3. Location of project, including coordinates

1

JCM_ID_F_PDD_ver01.0

Country	Republic of Indonesia
Region/State/Province etc.:	West Java Province
City/Town/Community etc:	Kelurahan Bantargebang, Kecamatan Bantargebang, Bekasi
Latitude, longitude	6°18'33.9"S, 106°59'02.8"E

A.4. Name of project participants

The Republic of Indonesia	PT. Adib Global Food Supplies, PT. Mayekawa Indonesia
Japan	MAYEKAWA MFG. CO., LTD.

A.5. Duration

Starting date of project operation	18/12/2014
Expected operational lifetime of project	12years

A.6. Contribution from developed countries

The proposed project was partially supported by the Ministry of the Environment, Japan through the financing programme for JCM model projects which provided financial supports up to 50% of initial investment for the projects in order to acquire JCM credits. As for technology transfer, MAYEKAWA MFG. CO., LTD has conducted OJT training and provided a manual on operation, maintenance and safety measures of the facilities introduced to the project of PT. Adib Global Food Supplies. Maintenance services after project implementation will be provided by PT Mayekawa, which will also contribute to technical transfer through maintenance experiences of the staff of PT. Adib Global Food Supplies.

B. Application of an approved methodology(ies)

B.1. Selection of methodology(ies)

Selected approved methodology No.	ID_AM003
Version number	1.0
Selected approved methodology No.	N/A
Version number	N/A
Selected approved methodology No.	N/A
Version number	N/A

B.2. Explanation of how the project meets eligibility criteria of the approved methodology

2

JCM_ID_F_PDD_ver01.0

Eligibility criteria	Descriptions specified in the methodology	Project information
Criterion 1	The project installs cooling system at food industry cold storage and frozen food processing plants for the purpose of chilling the food products to below -20 deg. C.	The project installs cooling system at a food industry cold storage for the purpose of chilling the food products below -25 deg. C.
Criterion 2	The project system is a secondary loop cooling system using natural refrigerant. CO_2 is used as the secondary refrigerant in the system.	The project system is a secondary loop cooling system using natural refrigerant (NH_3 and CO_2). CO_2 is used as the secondary refrigerant in the system.
Criterion 3	The refrigerator applied in the project cooling system is a two stage compressor refrigerator with a cooling capacity as shown below: For cold storage: less than 340kW For individual quick freezer: less than 260kW	The refrigerator applied in the project cooling system is a two stage compressor refrigerator for cold storage with 189kW cooling capacity.
Criterion 4	The compressor of the project refrigerator is controlled by inverter.	The refrigerator installed under the project is NewTon R-6000 (HCS-90L-PR4I-01), and its compressor is controlled by an inverter.
Criterion 5	COP of the project refrigerator i ($COP_{PJ,i}$) is shown below: For cold storage: more than 2.0 For individual quick freezer: more than 1.5	The COP of the NewTon R-6000 (HCS-90L-PR4I-01) installed under the project is 2.20.
Criterion 6	Periodical check at least once a year is planned.	Periodical check is planned once a year.
Criterion 7	Plan for not releasing the primary refrigerant used for project refrigerator is prepared. In the case of replacing the existing refrigerator with the project refrigerator, refrigerant used for the existing refrigerator is not released	The plan for not releasing the primary refrigerant used in the project refrigerator has been prepared. As this is a Green field project, the existing refrigerator does not exist in the project site.

JCM_ID_F_PDD_ver01.0

	to the air.	

C. Calculation of emission reductions

C.1. All emission sources and their associated greenhouse gases relevant to the JCM project

Reference emissions	
Emission sources	GHG type
Electricity consumption by the reference refrigerator	CO2
Project emissions	
Emission sources	GHG type
Electricity consumption by the project refrigerator	CO2

C.2. Figure of all emission sources and monitoring points relevant to the JCM project

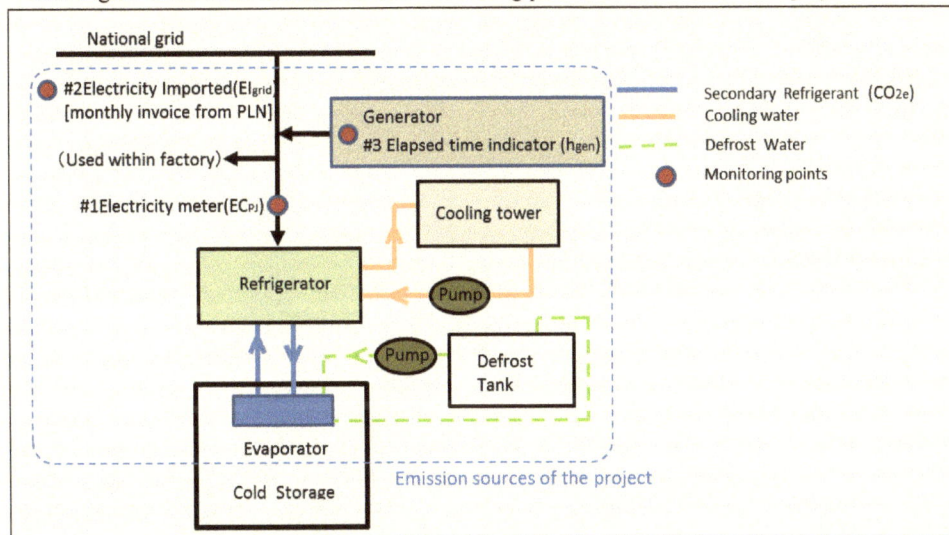

C.3. Estimated emissions reductions in each year

Year	Estimated Reference emissions (tCO$_{2e}$)	Estimated Project Emissions (tCO$_{2e}$)	Estimated Emission Reductions (tCO$_{2e}$)
2013	0	0	0
2014	24	19	5
2015	631	491	140
2016	631	491	140
2017	631	491	140

4

2018	631	491	140
2019	631	491	140
2020	631	491	140
Total (tCO$_{2e}$)	3,810	2,965	845

D. Environmental impact assessment

Legal requirement of environmental impact assessment for the proposed project	No

E. Local stakeholder consultation

E.1. Solicitation of comments from local stakeholders

The project activity is limited to installation of a new high efficient refrigerator in a new cold storage with a limited level of potential social and environmental impact. The PP identified local stakeholders as the local governments: Bekasi Regency Government and West Java Provincial Government as there is no residence within the area where any environmental impact may be caused by the proposed project.

The PP conducted a local stakeholder consultation meeting (face to face meeting) described as below:

[Date]   9:30 – 11:30   8th December 2014

[Venue]   Conference room of the West Java Provincial Government

[Agencies participated in the consultation]

No	Organization
1	International Cooperation Division, Regional Autonomy and Cooperation Bureau, Government of West Java Province
2	Department of Communications and Information, Government of West Java Province
3	Social Service Bureau, Government of West Java Province
4	Regional Environmental Management Board of West Java Province (BPLHD Jawa Barat)
5	Economic Bureau, Government of West Java Province
6	Fishery and Marine Department, Government of West Java Province
7	Agriculture and Food Crops Department, Government of West Java Province
8	Industry and Trade Department, Government of West Java Province

For the following agencies which were unable to attend the local stakeholder consultation meeting mentioned above, PP provided the distributed documents in the meeting to these

JCM_ID_F_PDD_ver01.0

agencies and requested them to provide their comments by email.

1) Regional Development Planning Board of West Java Province (BAPPEDA Jawa Barat)
2) Regional Environmental Agency of Bekasi Regency (BPLHD Kota Bekasi)

E.2. Summary of comments received and their consideration

Stakeholders	Comments received	Consideration of comments received
International Cooperation Division, Regional Autonomy and Cooperation Bureau, Government of West Java Province	We welcome the implementation of proposed projects under the JCM between Indonesia and Japan.	No action is needed.
	We support the promotion of the low carbon technologies. We hope there would be another chance for us to seek for other projects.	No action is needed.
Economic Bureau, Government of West Java Province	We are ready to support JCM project.	No action is needed.
Social Service Bureau, Government of West Java Province	This technology can contribute to Indonesia by its high efficiency. However, the price seems to be too high for the fishery communities and SMEs to consider using it. Financial support scheme for the communities or SMEs by Indonesian side needs to be considered.	No action is needed.

F. References

-

Reference lists to support descriptions in the PDD, if any.

JCM_ID_F_PDD_ver01.0

Annex
-

Revision history of PDD		
Version	Date	Contents revised
01.0	25/12/2014	First Edition
02.0	13/02/2015	Second Edition

Monitoring Plan Sheet (Input Sheet) [Attachment to Project Design Document]

Table 1: Parameters to be monitored ex post

(a) Monitoring point No.	(b) Parameters	(c) Description of data	(d) Estimated Values	(e) Units	(f) Monitoring option	(g) Source of data	(h) Measurement methods and procedures	(i) Monitoring frequency	(j) Other comments
(1)	$EC_{PJ,i,p}$	Amount of electricity consumption of the project refrigerator i during the period p	603.0	MWh/p	Option C	Monitored data	Data is measured by measuring equipments in the factory. - Specification of measuring equipments: Electrical power meter is applied for measurement of electrical power consumption of project refrigerator. - Measuring and recording: Measured data is automatically sent to a server where data is recorded and stored. - Data collection and reporting: Inputting the collected data to a spreadsheet electronically. - QA/QC: 1) Recorded data is checked its integrity once a month by responsible staff. 2) Calibration is conducted every year after the installation by a qualified entity.	Continuously	
(2)	$EI_{grid,p}$	Electricity imported from the grid to the project site during the period p	603.0	MWh/p	Option B	Invoice from the power company who owns the grid	Data is collected from relevant invoices from the power company who owns the grid and input to a spreadsheet electronically.	Every month	
(3)	$h_{gen,p}$	Operating time of captive electricity generator during the period p	0	hours/p	Option C	Monitored data	Data is measured by meter equipped to a generator. - Specification of measuring equipments: Meter is applied for measurement of the operation time of captive electricity generator. - Measuring and recording: Measured data is recorded and stored electronically. - Data collection and reporting: Inputting the collected data to a spreadsheet electronically. - QA/QC: 1) Recorded data is checked its integrity once a month by responsible staff. 2) Calibration is conducted every year after the installation by a qualified entity.	Continuously	

Table 2: Project-specific parameters to be fixed ex ante

(a) Parameters	(b) Description of data	(c) Estimated Values	(d) Units	(e) Source of data	(f) Other comments
EF_{elec}	[For grid electricity] CO_2 emission factor for consumed electricity	0.814	tCO_2/MWh	The most recent value available at the time of validation is applied and fixed for the monitoring period thereafter. The data is sourced from "Emission Factors of Electricity Interconnection Systems", National Committee on Clean Development Mechanism Indonesian DNA for CDM unless otherwise instructed by the Joint Committee.	
EF_{elec}	[For captive electricity] CO_2 emission factor for consumed electricity	0.80	tCO_2/MWh	Default value stipulated in the para.9 of CDM approved methodology AMS-I.A ver.16.	
$COP_{RE,i}$	COP of the project refrigerator type i	1.71	-	The default values for $COP_{RE,i}$ are set as follows: For cold storage: 1.71 For individual quick freezer: 1.32	
$COP_{PJ,i}$	COP of the reference refrigerator type i	2.20	-	Specifications of project refrigerator i prepared for the quotation or factory acceptance test data by manufacturer.	
RC_{gen}	Rated capacity of generator	200.00	kW	Specification of generator for captive electricity.	

Table3: *Ex-ante* estimation of CO_2 emission reductions

CO_2 emission reductions	Units
140	tCO_2/p

[Monitoring option]

Option A	Based on public data which is measured by entities other than the project participants (Data used: publicly recognized data such as statistical data and specifications)
Option B	Based on the amount of transaction which is measured directly using measuring equipments (Data used: commercial evidence such as invoices)
Option C	Based on the actual measurement using measuring equipments (Data used: measured values)

COP = coefficient of performance, MWh = megawatt-hour, tCO_2 = tons of carbon dioxide.

Monitoring Spreadsheet: JCM_ID_AM003_ver01.0

Sectoral scope: 03

Monitoring Plan Sheet (Calculation Process Sheet) [Attachment to Project Design Document]

1. Calculations for emission reductions	Fuel type	Value	Units	Parameter
Emission reductions during the period *p*	N/A	140.7	tCO_2/p	ER_p
2. Selected default values, etc.				
COP of the reference refrigerator type *i*	N/A	1.71	-	$COP_{RE,i}$
COP of the project refrigerator type *i*	N/A	2.20	-	$COP_{PJ,i}$
3. Calculations for reference emissions				
Reference emissions during the period *p*	N/A	631.5	tCO_2/p	RE_p
CO_2 emission factor for consumed electricity [grid]	Electricity	0.814	tCO_2/MWh	EF_{elec}
CO_2 emission factor for consumed electricity [captive]	Electricity	0.80	tCO_2/MWh	EF_{elec}
Proportion of grid electricity over total electricity consumed at the project site	N/A	1.00	-	-
Proportion of captive electricity over total electricity consumed at the project site	N/A	0.00	-	-
Amount of electricity consumption of the project refrigerator *i* during the period *p*	Electricity	603	MWh/p	$EC_{PJ,i,p}$
COP of the reference refrigerator type *i*	N/A	1.71	-	$COP_{RE,i}$
COP of the project refrigerator type *i*	N/A	2.20	-	$COP_{PJ,i}$
4. Calculations of the project emissions				
Project emissions during the period *p*		490.8	tCO_2/p	PE_p
CO_2 emission factor for consumed electricity [grid]	Electricity	0.814	tCO_2/MWh	EF_{elec}
CO_2 emission factor for consumed electricity [captive]	Electricity	0.80	tCO_2/MWh	EF_{elec}
Proportion of grid electricity over total electricity consumed at the project site	N/A	1.00	-	-
Proportion of captive electricity over total electricity consumed at the project site	N/A	0.00	-	-
Amount of electricity consumption of the project refrigerator *i* during the period *p*	Electricity	603	MWh/p	$EC_{PJ,i,p}$

[List of Default Values]

	$COP_{RE,i}$	
For cold storage	1.71	
For individual quick freezer	1.32	

COP = coefficient of performance, MWh = megawatt-hour, tCO_2 = tons of carbon dioxide.

Monitoring Spreadsheet: JCM_ID_AM003_ver01.0

Sectoral scope: 03

Monitoring Structure Sheet [Attachment to Project Design Document]

Responsible personnel	Role
Project Manager	Responsible for project implementation, monitoring results and reporting.
Deputy Project Manager	Appointed to be in charge of confirming the recorded data and archived data.
QA/QC team	Appointed to be in charge of checking the archived data for irregularity and calibration of the monitoring equipments.
Record keeper	Appointed to be in charge of inputting the monitored data to a spreadsheet (recording sheet) mannually

QA/QC = quality assurance and quality control.

Monitoring Spreadsheet: JCM_ID_AM003_ver01.0
Sectoral scope: 03

Monitoring Report Sheet (Input Sheet) [For Verification]

Table 1: Parameters monitored ex post

(a) Monitoring period	(b) Monitoring point No.	(c) Parameters	(d) Description of data	(e) Estimated Values	(f) Units	(g) Monitoring option	(h) Source of data	(i) Measurement methods and procedures	(j) Monitoring frequency	(k) Other comments
	(1)	$EC_{PJ,i,p}$	Amount of electricity consumption of the project refrigerator i during the period p		MWh/p	Option C	Monitored data	Data is measured by measuring equipments in the factory. - Specification of measuring equipments: Electrical power meter is applied for measurement of electrical power consumption of project refrigerator. - Measuring and recording: Measured data is automatically sent to a server where data is recorded and stored. - Data collection and reporting: Inputting the recorded data to a spreadsheet electrically. - QA/QC: 1) Recorded data is checked its integrity once a month by responsible staff. 2) Calibration is conducted every year after the installation by a qualified entity.	Continuously	
	(2)	$EI_{grid,p}$	Electricity imported from the grid to the project site during the period p		MWh/p	Option B or Option C	Invoice from the power company for Option B or monitored data for Option C	[for Option B] Data is collected and recorded from invoices from the power company. [for Option C] Data is measured by measuring equipments in the factory. - Specification of measuring equipments: Electrical power meter is applied for measurement of electrical power consumption of project refrigerator. - Measuring and recording: Measured data is automatically sent to a server where data is recorded and stored. - Data collection and reporting: Inputting the recorded data to a spreadsheet electrically. - QA/QC: 1) Recorded data is checked its integrity once a month by responsible staff. 2) Calibration is conducted every year after the installation by a qualified entity.	Every month	
	(3)	$h_{gen,p}$	Operating time of captive electricity generator during the period p		hours/p	Option C	Monitored data	Data is measured by meter equipped to a generator. - Specification of measuring equipments: Meter is applied for measurement of the operation time of captive electricity generator. - Measuring and recording: Measured data is recorded and stored electrically. - Data collection and reporting: Inputting the recorded data to a spreadsheet electrically. - QA/QC: 1) Recorded data is checked its integrity once a month by responsible staff. 2) Calibration is conducted every year after the installation by a qualified entity.	Continuously	

Table 2: Project-specific parameters fixed ex ante

(a) Parameters	(b) Description of data	(c) Estimated Values	(d) Units	(e) Source of data	(f) Other comments
EF_{elec}	[For grid electricity] CO_2 emission factor for consumed electricity	0.814	tCO_2/MWh	The most recent value available at the time of validation is applied and fixed for the monitoring period thereafter. The data is sourced from "Emission Factors of Electricity Interconnection Systems", National Committee on Clean Development Mechanism Indonesian DNA for CDM unless otherwise instructed by the Joint Committee.	
EF_{elec}	[For captive electricity] CO_2 emission factor for consumed electricity	0.800	tCO_2/MWh	Default value stipulated in the para.9 of CDM approved methodology AMS-I.A ver.16.	
$COP_{RE,i}$	COP of the project refrigerator type i	1.710	-	The default values for $COP_{RE,i}$ are set as follows: For cold storage: 1.71 For individual quick freezer: 1.32	
$COP_{PJ,i}$	COP of the reference refrigerator type i	2.200	-	Specifications of project refrigerator i prepared for the quotation or factory acceptance test data by manufacturer.	
RC_{gen}	Rated capacity of generator	200.000	kW	Specification of generator for captive electricity.	

Table3: *Ex-post* calculation of CO_2 emission reductions

Monitoring Period	CO_2 emission reductions	Units
	#DIV/0!	tCO_2/p

[Monitoring option]

Option A	Based on public data which is measured by entities other than the project participants (Data used: publicly recognized data such as statistical data and specifications)
Option B	Based on the amount of transaction which is measured directly using measuring equipments (Data used: commercial evidence such as invoices)
Option C	Based on the actual measurement using measuring equipments (Data used: measured values)

COP = coefficient of performance, MWh = megawatt-hour, tCO_2 = tons of carbon dioxide.

Monitoring Spreadsheet: JCM_ID_AM003_ver01.0

Sectoral scope: 03

Monitoring Report Sheet (Calculation Process Sheet) [For Verification]

1. Calculations for emission reductions	Fuel type	Value	Units	Parameter
Emission reductions during the period p	N/A	#DIV/0!	tCO_2/p	ER_p
2. Selected default values, etc.				
COP of the reference refrigerator type i	N/A	1.71	-	$COP_{RE,i}$
COP of the project refrigerator type i	N/A	2.20	-	$COP_{PJ,i}$
3. Calculations for reference emissions				
Reference emissions during the period p	N/A	#DIV/0!	tCO_2/p	RE_p
CO_2 emission factor for consumed electricity [grid]	Electricity	0.814	tCO_2/MWh	EF_{elec}
CO_2 emission factor for consumed electricity [captive]	Electricity	0.80	tCO_2/MWh	EF_{elec}
Proportion of grid electricity over total electricity consumed at the project site	N/A	#DIV/0!	-	-
Proportion of captive electricity over total electricity consumed at the project site	N/A	#DIV/0!	-	-
Amount of electricity consumption of the project refrigerator i during the period p	Electricity	0	MWh/p	$EC_{PJ,i,p}$
COP of the reference refrigerator type i	N/A	1.71	-	$COP_{RE,i}$
COP of the project refrigerator type i	N/A	2.20	-	$COP_{PJ,i}$
4. Calculations of the project emissions				
Project emissions during the period p		#DIV/0!	tCO_2/p	PE_p
CO_2 emission factor for consumed electricity [grid]	Electricity	0.814	tCO_2/MWh	EF_{elec}
CO_2 emission factor for consumed electricity [captive]	Electricity	0.80	tCO_2/MWh	EF_{elec}
Proportion of grid electricity over total electricity consumed at the project site	N/A	#DIV/0!	-	-
Proportion of captive electricity over total electricity consumed at the project site	N/A	#DIV/0!	-	-
Amount of electricity consumption of the project refrigerator i during the period p	Electricity	0	MWh/p	$EC_{PJ,i,p}$

[List of Default Values]

	$COP_{RE,i}$	
For cold storage	1.71	
For individual quick freezer	1.32	

COP = coefficient of performance, MWh = megawatt-hour, tCO_2 = tons of carbon dioxide.

Supporting Documentation

Evidence 2

NH$_3$/CO$_2$ cooling system

NewTon

Forwarding to the future refrigeration systems

Realizing more advanced economics and energy-saving

The world's first introduction of semi-hermetic IPM motor to be mounted on ammonia screw compressor

Interior Permanent Magnet (IPM) motor

In order to improve the drive efficiency the system employs IPM motor, achieving higher efficiency by 5 to 10 % than conventional induction type.

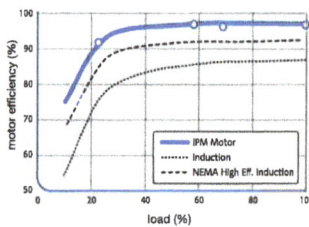

Revolution speed control by Variable Frequency Drive (VFD)

VFDs are used as driver to drive IPM motor. The rated revolution is set 4,500rpm (partially 5,600rpm) and continuously revolution speed control is equipped as a standard feature to correspond to part load operation. Driving at high speed and controlling revolution speed greatly contribute to energy-saving part load operation as compared to the conventional slide valve type.

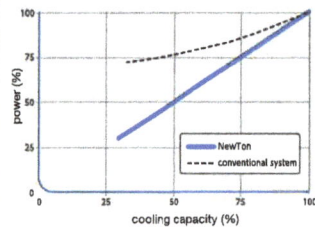

New Profile

We developed a new profile for rotors with advanced machining technology enabling it to reduce internal leakage and achieve higher efficiency.

Graph: motor efficiency (%) vs load (%) — IPM Motor, Induction, NEMA High Eff. Induction

Graph: power (%) vs cooling capacity (%) — NewTon, conventional system

new rotors

Adopted shell & plate type heat exchanger

We employed compact and high performance shell & plate heat exchangers on both condenser and evaporator to enable them to exchange heat even with a small differential temperature.

Minimizing ammonia charge

Employing indirect cooling method enables ammonia to be contained only in a machine room, plus ammonia charge volume in this product 25kg to max. 75kg for each package.

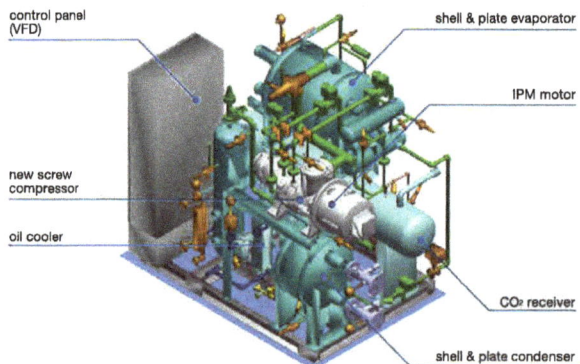

control panel (VFD)

shell & plate evaporator

IPM motor

new screw compressor

oil cooler

CO$_2$ receiver

shell & plate condenser

Evidence for Criterion 2 (secondary loop cooling system using natural refrigerant)

Indirect cooling method utilizing carbon dioxide (CO_2) characteristics

NewTon system can contain ammonia completely only in machine room so that it can achieve both energy-saving and safety.

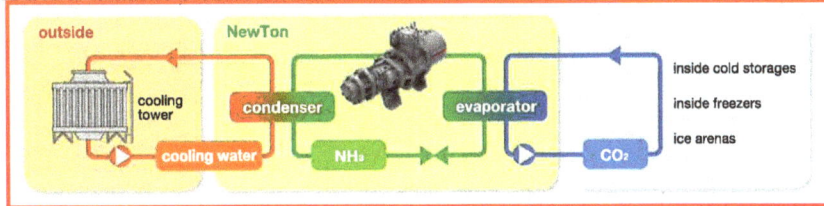

Over 30% energy-saving

Tokyo Toyomi Cold Storage Funabashi Logistic center

capacity (ton)	after construction (year)	previous equipment refrigerant	previous equipment compressor	the number of NewTon units (unit)	Reducing rate of consumption electricity (%)
18,000	29	HCFC-22	Screw	8	31.1

Comparison of before and after introducing NewTon

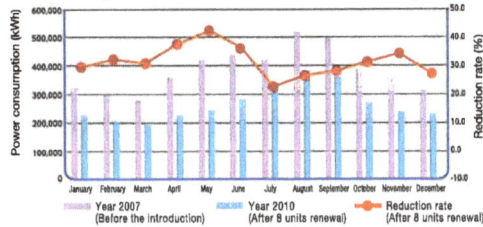

* estimation from the power company bills
* all electricity including main machine, auxiliary machine, transporting machine, lighting and etc.

Evidence for Criterion 3-5:

For Cold storages and Ice plants NewTon R   NewTon C

		NewTon R-3000	NewTon R-6000	NewTon R-8000	NewTon C
CO₂ supply temperature			-32°C		-5°C
cooling capacity		94.5kW	189kW	270kW	235kW
motor kW		43kW	86kW (43kW × 2)	120kW	65kW
C.O.P (EER)		2.2			2.25
power source	for motor	AC400/440V × 50/60Hz	AC400/440V × 50/60Hz	AC400/440V × 50/60Hz	AC400/440V × 50/60Hz
	for control	AC200/220V × 50/60Hz	AC200/220V × 50/60Hz	AC200/220V × 50/60Hz	AC200/220V × 50/60Hz
refrigerant			primary: NH₃		
compressor	type		semi-hermetic compound screw		semi-hermetic single stage screw
	drive method		VFD		
	motor type		IPM motor		
ammonia charge		25kg	50kg	75kg	60kg
outer dimensions		L2,780 × W1,950 × H2,400 mm	L4,725 × W2,378 × H2,600 mm	L3,950 × W2,550 × H2,650 mm	L3,400 × W2,200 × H2,700 mm
net weight		3,300kg	6,800kg	7,600kg	6,000kg

in the case of cooling water at 32°C

VFD: Variable-frequency drive (inverter)

For Freezers NewTon F

		NewTon F-300	NewTon F-600	NewTon F-800
CO₂ supply temperature			-42°C	
cooling capacity		70kW	140kW	170kW
motor kW		43kW	86kW (43kW × 2)	100kW
power source	for motor	AC400/440V × 50/60Hz	AC400/440V × 50/60Hz	AC400/440V × 50/60Hz
	for control	AC200/220V × 50/60Hz	AC200/220V × 50/60Hz	AC200/220V × 50/60Hz
refrigerant			primary: NH₃	
compressor	type		semi-hermetic compound screw	
	drive method		VFD	
	motor type		IPM motor	
ammonia charge		25kg	50kg	75kg
outer dimensions		L2,780 × W1,950 × H2,400 mm	L4,725 × W2,378 × H2,800 mm	L3,950 × W2,550 × H2,650 mm
net weight		3,300kg	6,800kg	7,600kg

in the case of cooling water at 32°C

For Ice arenas NewTon S

		NewTon S
CO₂ supply temperature		-11°C
cooling capacity		185kW
motor kW		63kW
power source	for motor	AC400/440V × 50/60Hz
	for control	AC200/220V × 50/60Hz
refrigerant		primary: NH₃
compressor	type	semi-hermetic single stage screw
	drive method	VFD
	motor type	IPM motor
ammonia charge		60kg
outer dimensions		L3,400 × W2,200 × H2,700 mm
net weight		6,000kg

in the case of cooling water at 32°C

MAYEKAWA MYCOM

MAYEKAWA MFG. CO., LTD.
3-14-15 Botan Koto-ku, Tokyo 135-8482, JAPAN
TEL:(81)-3-3642-8181 FAX:(81)-3-3643-7094
http://www.mayekawa.com/

Subject to change without notice.

Cat.No.PD046 01101210 -12.10. Printed in Japan.

JCM_ID_F_MoC_ver01.0

JCM Modalities of Communication Statement Form

Section 1: Project description	
Title of the project	Project of Introducing High Efficiency Refrigerator to a Food Industry Cold Storage in Indonesia
Country	Republic of Indonesia
Date of Submission	25/12/2014

Section 2: Nomination of focal point entity(ies)		
Name of entity: MAYEKAWA MFG. CO., LTD.		
Address (incl. postcode): 3-14-15, Botan, Koto-Ku, Tokyo 135-8482, Japan		
Telephone: +81-3-3642-6005		**Fax: +81-3-3642-2815**
E-mail:		**Website: http://www.mayekawa.com**
Primary authorised signatory:	Mr. ☒	Ms. ☐
Last name: Maekawa		**First name: Tadashi**
Title: President		
Specimen signature:		Date: 18/12/2014
Alternate authorised signatory:	Mr. ☒	Ms. ☐
Last name: Takahashi		**First name: Shigeru**
Title: Director		
Specimen signature:		Date: 18/12/2014
Contact person:	Mr. ☒	Ms. ☐
Last name: Mogi		**First name: Osamu**
Title: Assistant General Manager		
Department: Global Project Sales Group		
Mobile: +81-80-1217-7451		**Direct tel.: +81-3-3642-6005**
E-mail: osamu-mogi@mayekawa.co.jp		**Direct fax: +81-3-3642-2815**

USE THIS SECTION FOR POST-REGISTRATION SUBMISSIONS ONLY	Is this entity changing its name?	Yes ☐ (Former entity name:) No ☐
	Is the entity also a project participant?	Yes ☐ No ☐
	If the entity is also a project participant, do the same signatories represent it in its project participant role?	Yes ☐ No ☐

I

Name of the TPE that conducts validation (and verification) for the project:	Japan Quality Assurance organization	
Address (incl. postcode): 1-25, Kandasudacho, Chiyoda-ku, Tokyo, 101-8555, Japan		
Contact person:	Mr. ☒	Ms. ☐
Last name: Motokawa	First name: Hiroshi	
Title: Manager		
Department: CDM Assessment Division, Global Environment Department		
E-mail: motokawa-hiroshi@jqa.jp	Telephone: 03-4560-5526	

Section 4: List of project participants other than nominated focal point entity(ies)	
	Name of project participant
(1)	PT ADIB GLOBAL FOOD SUPPLIES
(2)	PT MAYEKAWA INDONESIA
(3)	
(4)	
(5)	
(6)	

*Rows may be added, as needed
*Contact information of each participant is indicated in Section 5.

JCM_ID_F_Reg_Req_ver01.0

JCM Project Registration Request Form

List of documents to be attached to this form *(Please check to confirm)*	PDD (latest version)	☒	
	MoC	☒	
	Validation report	☒	
Reference number	ID002		
Title of the project	Project of Introducing High Efficiency Refrigerator to a Food Industry Cold Storage in Indonesia		
Focal point entity	MAYEKAWA MFG. CO., LTD.		
Third-party entity (TPE)	Japan Quality Assurance organization		
Applied methodology	No.	ID_AM003	
	Version	1.0	
	Title	Installation of Energy-efficient Refrigerators Using Natural Refrigerant at Food Industry Cold Storage and Frozen Food Processing Plant	
	Sectoral scope	03	

Name of the focal point entity:	MAYEKAWA MFG. CO., LTD.	
Authorised signatory:	Mr. ☒	Ms. ☐
Last name: Takahashi	**First name:** Shigeru	
Title: Assistant General Manager		
Specimen signature:		**Date:** 06/03/2015

[Signature by the focal point of the project participants as appeared on the MoC]

*Tables should be added, if more than one focal point are designated.

APPENDIX 8:
INFORMATION SOURCES

Guidelines, templates, and requirements for preparing Joint Crediting Mechanism (JCM) methodology can be found on the JCM website: https://www.jcm.go.jp/rules_and_guidelines. In addition, each host country has its own website where project proponents can find all necessary information about methodologies, such as the list of approved methodologies, guidelines on developing a proposed methodology, and a methodology proposal form, among others.

List of Specific Host Country Joint Crediting Mechanism Websites

Host Country	Website
Mongolia	www.jcm.go.jp/mn-jp
Bangladesh	www.jcm.go.jp/bd-jp
Ethiopia	www.jcm.go.jp/et-jp
Kenya	www.jcm.go.jp/ke-jp
Maldives	www.jcm.go.jp/mv-jp
Viet Nam	www.jcm.go.jp/vn-jp
Lao People's Democratic Republic	www.jcm.go.jp/la-jp
Indonesia	www.jcm.go.jp/id-jp
Costa Rica	www.jcm.go.jp/cr-jp
Palau	www.jcm.go.jp/pw-jp
Cambodia	www.jcm.go.jp/kh-jp
Mexico	www.jcm.go.jp/mx-jp
Saudi Arabia	www.jcm.go.jp/sa-jp
Chile	www.jcm.go.jp/cl-jp
Myanmar	www.jcm.go.jp/mm-jp
Thailand	www.jcm.go.jp/th-jp

Other sources:

Projects and studies about the JCM and JCM methodologies are published on the JCM website of the Global Environment Centre Foundation (GEC): http://gec.jp/jcm/projects/index.html

Clean Development Mechanism (CDM) methodologies can be used as reference sources to develop JCM methodologies. Approved CDM methodologies can be found on the official UNFCCC website: https://cdm.unfccc.int/methodologies/PAmethodologies/approved

www.ingramcontent.com/pod-product-compliance
Lightning Source LLC
Chambersburg PA
CBHW041120280326
41928CB00061B/3469